NURSE SARAH ANNE

NURSE
SARAH ANNE

With Florence Nightingale
at Scutari

Edited with an Introduction and Notes
by ROBERT G. RICHARDSON

With a Foreword
by CHARLES HUGH TERROT

JOHN MURRAY

Printed in Great Britain
by W & J Mackay Limited, Chatham
0 7195 3385 6

FOREWORD

When Sarah Anne was a child, it probably never entered her mind that one day she might become a nurse. She was raised in an atmosphere of impeccable upper class respectability and wealth. At the time of her birth in 1822, her father, Charles Hughes Terrot, was a clergyman with a comfortable living at Berwick-on-Tweed; educated at Winchester and Cambridge, where he was awarded the Seatonian Prize, he was considered to have a brilliant future.

The Terrot family is of Huguenot ancestry. The first, Jean Charles de Terrot, fled to Amsterdam at the time of the Edict of Nantes. His estate had been in the Basse Normandie and, being of the 'petite noblesse' of France, he was given a commission in the army of William of Orange in the crack Holstein Regiment. When William III came to England in 1688, Charles de Terrot was posted to Dublin and seconded to the English Army. After a time, he dropped the 'de' from the family name, wishing to be regarded as an Englishman. Since then, successive generations of Terrots have served their country in a number of capacities (mainly in the Army and the Church), some with considerable distinction. Ranking very highly amongst them is surely Sarah Anne.

Although Charles Hughes Terrot became a bishop at an early age, his main interests throughout life were pure mathematics and economics. As an ecclesiastic, he solved many complex financial problems for the Church as a whole. By all accounts he was a quiet, kindly man who had been brought up by his mother; his father, a young army lieutenant, was killed in India before he was born. Charles Hughes married a Miss Diana Woods, who in due course persuaded her husband to move to Edinburgh. She had ten children in quick succession and died young. Eight of these children were girls, one of the sons died in infancy, and the second son was killed in the Indian Mutiny. Sarah Anne was the second eldest child. Her upbringing was left almost entirely in the hands of an excellent governess and it was she who inspired Sarah Anne to take an interest in nursing, nurses and their patients. Sarah Anne was an attractive, vivacious girl who became dedicated to the cause of helping the underprivileged in the Edinburgh slums, until she told her father, by then Bishop of Edinburgh, that she wished to become a nurse.

In that era, most fathers holding positions in high office would have been horrified at the idea of a daughter becoming a nurse, but the Bishop took the news fairly calmly and pro-mised to 'explore the possibilities' in the most respectable context possible. It so happened that he had a close friend, Dr. Pusey, who was a distinguished theologian, deeply concerned with the problems of sick and destitute people. He wrote to Dr. Pusey: 'My daughter, Sarah Anne, has a desire for greater use and with intimate communication with the sick and poor, working with women whom she can look to as real followers of Christ.'

Dr. Pusey answered that he knew of a certain Miss Sellon, daughter of a Naval commander, who fairly recently had founded a sisterhood at Devonport with the primary object of caring for the welfare of orphans, but he added that in addition to this work, the sisters undertook a certain amount of nursing, particularly during the cholera epidemics which frequently broke out in Plymouth and Devonport.

In 1847, Sarah Anne entered the Sellon Order as a 'child'—

that is to say, a novice on probation. But because of her out-
standing nursing ability, which soon became evident, she was
quickly promoted to the status of 'Sister', then 'Eldress'.

Sarah Anne was one of the eight Sellons chosen to join
Florence Nightingale's expedition to the Crimea, and her journal which follows covers the first few months of this momen-
tous undertaking. After Sarah Anne's return from the Crimea
in the spring of 1855, there is a most unfortunate gap of 43
years in a full knowledge of her activities. The reason for this
is twofold. Despite Florence Nightingale's epic achievements
in the field of nursing, nurses were *still* looked down upon and
few members of my family bothered to record in writing any
comments of how Sarah Anne spent her time. I cannot trace a
single obituary notice. Secondly, all her correspondence (including letters from Charles Dickens) was lost in a blitz during
World War II when a train carrying a box of Terrot family
'treasures' to the comparative safety of Scotland was bombed.
To the best of my knowledge there is not even a single letter
of hers in existence.

One fact is quite certain: Sarah Anne returned from Scutari
with permanently impaired health. For a time she worked as a
nurse in St. Thomas's Hospital, and I have read the reports on
her written by the Matron of that day which show that she was
suffering from ill-health. She then went back to the family
home in Edinburgh to look after her father who had been
ailing for some time. Her surviving sisters were living in
Australia and Canada so there was no one else to look after the
ageing bishop.

After his death in 1872, she sold up the family home, an
imposing mansion, No. 9 Carlton Terrace, which is still standing, and shared a much smaller house with a niece named
Annie Malcolm. It is believed that she undertook a certain
amount of welfare work in the Edinburgh slums.

While her father was still alive and for the next twenty years,
she made frequent visits to Tong Castle in Shropshire, which
was leased by the Earl of Bradford to close Terrot relatives

named Hartley. This magnificent castle no longer exists and has been razed to the ground. It was here that she met another guest, Charles Dickens, and listened enraptured to his recitals. Apparently the interest was mutual. Dickens recognized her worth as an individual and a warm friendship sprang up between them.

Another friendship she made was with my great-uncle, Thorneycroft Hartley, who in 1879 and in 1880 won the All England men's tennis championship at Wimbledon. Sarah Anne followed 'tennis form' avidly; as a small boy, I heard this fact direct from my great-uncle, and I have a distinct memory of him saying that Sarah Anne had an extraordinary exuberance, was devoted to children, and also had a wry sense of humour; at any rate I feel that sense of humour shines like a fine thread through the hideous drama of pain, tragic heroism and official incompetence which her journal reveals.

My great grandmother, Alice Maria Terrot, was also a close friend. Her evocative account of Sarah Anne's investiture of the Royal Red Cross by Queen Victoria at Balmoral Castle in 1897 is included in this book. Alice herself was an interesting person. She was half French by birth, and was descended from one of the great French families, the de Sevracs. At one time she was engaged to Alfred Lord Tennyson, but the engagement was terminated on account of her extremely volatile temperament which was too much for the famous poet!

Sarah Anne died of heart disease in 1902. Her passing was barely noted by the majority of the Terrot family. But, unknown to them, she left behind a magnificent self-created memorial: her Journal.

CHARLES HUGH TERROT

CONTENTS

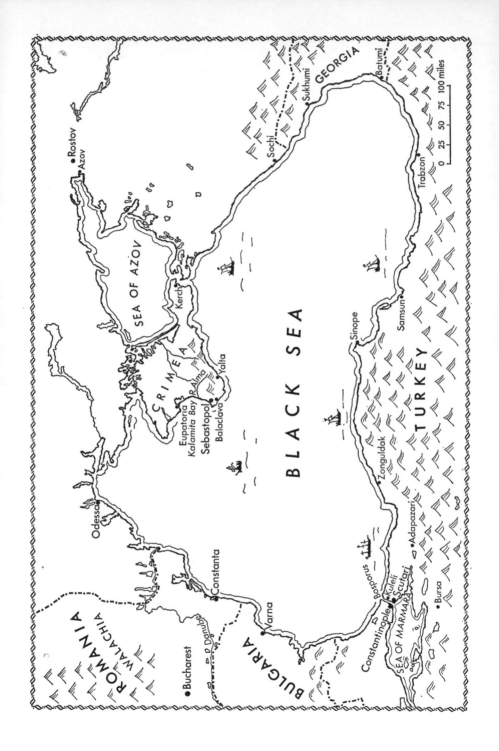

ILLUSTRATIONS

* *Reproduced by courtesy of the National Army Museum*

11

SETTING THE SCENE

PERSPECTIVE

Sarah Anne wrote from the heart. And that is what makes her journal probably the closest we can now come to understanding the reality of that terrible winter of 1854–5 when the inadequacies and incompetences of an old order were starkly exposed in the hospitals at Scutari. Unlike so many of those whose view of the Crimean War was committed to paper, she was free of the need to defend or attack a system. She was simply keeping a diary for herself; at first a day by day record of a new adventure but gradually, as she began to tell of the suffering and courage, time and self fell away and what had started as something personal became so much more. It is, unlike William Howard Russell's[1] rather contrived reports of human suffering, a compassionate document.

Sarah Anne Terrot was one of eight Sellonite Sisters in the small group of women who went with Florence Nightingale to Scutari in November 1854—their task, to nurse the soldiers of a British army that was in the process of being destroyed by disease. The Sellonites, an Anglican Order, proved the most valuable of this diverse collection of 'nurses' as they had already had experience of epidemics of cholera in the slums of Plymouth and were thus prepared, to some extent at least, for what they would find in the hospitals. In contrast, the experience of five of the Roman Catholic nuns was limited to caring for orphans at Norwood in south-east London.

The reason for Florence Nightingale taking her party to Turkey lay in one of W. H. Russell's despatches, published in *The Times* on October 13. In the English army, he wrote, 'there are no dressers or nurses to carry out the surgeons' directions, and to attend on the sick during the intervals between his visits. Here the French are greatly our superiors. Their medical arrangements are extremely good, their surgeons more numerous and they also have the help of the Sisters of Charity.' This aroused the British public and there was an indignant outcry at Russell's complimentary reference to the French. That would never do! Allies they might be now, but it was they who had been defeated at Waterloo. And anyway, a correspondent asked in *The Times* the next day, why were there no nurses in England like the Sisters of Charity, ready to serve wherever they were needed?

The fact that there *were* Sisters of Charity, both Anglican and Roman Catholic serves only to underline the fact that nursing in mid-Victorian England made but an insignificant contribution to the welfare of the people. To understand why, we must forget everything we know about the nurses and nursing of today. Women have always tended to the needs of the sick, but at no time were they taught the skills of nursing— the concept of the trained nurse is very much a modern one, and owes its inception to the genius of Florence Nightingale. Both social and religious considerations have been potent influences for good and bad on the care of the sick, and England, after the Reformation, fared worse than Catholic countries.

But it was not this particular despatch of Russell's that moved Miss Nightingale. She had already appreciated the need and for about a week had been arranging, on her own initiative, for a party of nurses to go to Scutari. After seventeen years of uncertainty and discouragement, the Crimea had shown her the direction her life's work was to take. What Russell's despatch and the consequent public outburst did achieve for her, was Government backing. On October 15 Sidney Herbert, the Secretary at War, wrote to her '. . . the deficiency of female nurses is undoubted, none but male nurses having ever been admitted to military hospitals.[2]

'It would be impossible to carry about a large staff of female nurses with the Army in the field. But at Scutari, having now a fixed hospital, no military reason exists against their introduction, and I am confident they might be introduced with great benefit, for hospital orderlies must be very rough hands, and most of them, on such an occasion as this, very inexperienced ones.'[3]

Russell's alarming despatches awakened the British public to the fact that all was not well in the Crimea. But just how bad was the situation? Forty years had passed since Waterloo and, except for the Empire-building campaigns in remote parts of Asia and Africa, they had been forty years of peace. The British public did not know what to expect—it certainly was not prepared for the harsh truths of war and the even more ghastly ravages of disease. Moreover, the invention of the telegraph had created a sense of immediacy never before experienced with a foreign campaign—public opinion could alter the course of events.

Russell knew this, and he pulled no punches. If he was to make an impact that would result in action, he could not afford to: 'No sufficient preparations have been made for the care of the wounded. Not only are there not sufficient surgeons . . . not only are there no dressers and nurses . . . there is not even linen to make bandages.' And then singling out the Army Medical Department for special attention: 'It is found that the commonest appliances of a workhouse sick ward are wanting, and that the men must die through the medical staff of the British Army having forgotten that old rags are necessary for the dressing of wounds.'

But Russell was painting only the side of the picture he saw. On October 20, 1854, just a week after this report was published, a letter from Dr. John Hall, the Inspector General in the Crimean area, reached his superior in London, Dr. Andrew Smith. In this he said he had been to Scutari and had 'much satisfaction in being able to state that the whole hospital establishment has now been put on a very creditable footing, and that the sick are all doing as well as could possibly be expected'.[4]

The perplexity of Dr. Smith, Director General of the Army Medical Department, was further increased when he received a letter from the dispenser at Scutari saying that the surgeons in charge of the wards were 'willing to assert publicly that no one under their care suffered from want of any stores. I further emphatically say that an assertion that I had not a supply of lint, linen, bandages, dressings and necessary medicines sufficient for any emergency would be unfounded'.[5]

Smith himself saw no reason to doubt this letter. Why should he? 'No-one', he later wrote to Hall in January, 1855, 'can look over the long and full lists of medicines, medical comforts, etc. which have been sent to Scutari during the last six months without being convinced that there must be an ample supply at that station for the wants of the whole Army'.[6]

So where did the truth lie? A clue that it depended very much on attitude and experience comes in a letter written on January 1, 1855, by a young assistant surgeon, E. M. Wrench, from Balaclava: 'Last week I had two letters from Scutari—the first was from a man who had *not* been out here [i.e. Balaclava], he described it as very uncomfortable, and a horrid place; the other was from Hervey Ludlow who *has* been out here and sent to Scutari invalided—he writes that it is a sort of Paradise compared to Balaclava.'[7]

The official record of events in the Crimea is enshrined in the painstakingly compiled records of the various Government commissions. Here again attitudes are in evidence, as when Mr. Ward, the 67-year-old Purveyor at Scutari, questioned there by the members of the Hospitals Commission in December, 1854, replied that though he had served through the whole of the Peninsular War 'the patients never were nearly so comfortable as they are here . . . Even when we returned to our own country from Walcheren and Corunna the comforts they got were by no means equal to what we have here'.[8]

But in England, where a tide of humanitarianism was already on the flood, comparisons with the Napoleonic Wars were just as invalid as they would be today and Russell's message was falling on the ears of a people ready to listen. He may have been guilty of exaggeration and distortion; he may not have appreciated the difficulties created by outworn regulations that crippled initiative; but what he wrote came as the truth day after day to the breakfast tables of the nation.

Over the years the facts of the Crimean War have been unravelled, and even the reasons for the catastrophic happenings, both military and medical (the two were closely interwoven), are now reasonably clear. The newspaper reports and the evidence before the commissions reflect the attitudes of the writers—either the horror at the unspeakable conditions expressed by those who were ignorant of what to expect, or the defensive positions taken by those who believed in the inevitability of it all but were swamped by the sheer magnitude of the disaster. Both were right in their way because the Crimea was the flash-point where so many old traditions came into conflict with progress, and the human element in consequence became hopelessly confused.

Yet, in spite of all the undoubted deficiencies, the hospitals at Scutari would almost certainly have been able to cope (according to early 19th-century standards) had the rot not already set in at the front; the hospitals were the end point in the line of evacuation. Their staff inherited the consequences of disaster elsewhere, but instead of meeting the crisis as a challenge, they stubbornly played the game according to the regulations. Nevertheless they were not alone in this, as the response of virtually everyone in authority in the whole theatre of war was obtuse beyond belief. It was not conflict with the Russian enemy that so nearly destroyed the British army; it was disease. Cholera. Dysentery. Typhus. Scurvy. Gangrene. And the aggravation of cold, exposure, and malnutrition. Infectious diseases, the curse of armies for centuries were still mysterious unknown quantities, and without a knowledge of their cause, control was a haphazard business. Although sanitation and hygiene were acquiring an aura of respectability, the reasons were charitable and empirical; thus they were easily ignored in conditions where rigid enforcement held the sole hope of salvation. The discovery of bacteria lay only a decade in the future, but it might just as well have been a million years.

Looking back from our privileged position, there was a terrible inevitability about the whole Crimean episode. So many different threads were being drawn to a close. In particular the fluctuating story of nursing care and the evolution of the Army Medical Department were both reaching a climax. A catharsis was desperately sought and that first ghastly winter in the Crimea became the chosen time and place. The outcome for the British was staggering—particularly as the winter of 1854–5 (the period covered by Sarah Anne's journal) is usually equated in people's minds with conditions throughout the whole war. Out of the opening chaos came an improvement that was scarcely believable, while the French army—whose medical services had been held up as an example—gathered throughout the war the highest sickness rate in history.

THE NURSES

The sick, like the poor, have always been with us and caring for them has been an integral part of existence. Yet the emergence of nursing as a highly trained profession began little more than a hundred years ago. In the middle of the 19th century, 'nursing' was in the hands of a pretty miscellaneous collection of women who between them looked after the physical and spiritual needs of the sick. They had in common their sex and a lack of special training for the work. They differed in their religious persuasions and in the fervour with which they tried to obtain converts—the sick patient was considered particularly susceptible to indoctrination; indeed the soul was often ministered to at the expense of treating the body. And bedevilling the entire structure of nursing, nurses, and the nursed was social class.

All the different faces of nursing at this period are met in Sarah Anne's journal. There was the professional nurse, whose shocking reputation for drunkenness, immorality, coarseness, and bad language is not to be wondered at, considering that she often came from the lowest strata of Victorian society and had to work extremely long hours in depressing and deplorable conditions. She was personified by Sarah Gamp; yet despite Dickens's assurances in the later editions of *Martin Chuzzlewit* that he had drawn Mrs. Gamp from life, the paid nurse was not always so vile—her character suffered at the hands of reforming zealots. Florence Nightingale, a most astute observer, saw her other side (though admittedly she was referring to those who had passed the selection for service in the military hospitals of the Crimea). 'Nurses' she wrote,[9] 'are careful, efficient, often decorous, and always kind, sometimes drunken, sometimes unchaste.' And when at first this type of nurse disappeared from the hospital wards, the patients, particularly the men, felt they had lost a point of contact with their own familiar world outside.

Nursing in hospital was done by these professional nurses though their duties amounted to little more than a specialized form of domestic service; most of what today would be regarded as nursing responsibilities were carried out by the doctors and medical students. For instance, doctors would change dressings, apply poultices, and give enemas—temperature, pulse, blood pressure, and respiration charts and other aspects of modern nursing routine were in any case non-existent.

The hospital was the nurse's home. Her bed was usually in the ward with the women patients or in a cubby-hole off the men's ward, but sometimes she might sleep in the attic or basement. She could be on duty for twenty-four or even forty-eight hours at a stretch and would cook her meals in the ward kitchen. She learnt her job by carrying out the doctors' orders, but promotion rarely came her way. The ward sisters (not to be confused with the Sisters of religious Orders—though the title did originate from this source) were usually better-class widows of respectable character whom circumstance had forced into earning a living. They were responsible for the running of their wards, for seeing that the nurses behaved themselves and that the doctors' instructions were carried out.

At the opposite pole to the professional nurses were the 'Ladies', the voluntary workers of good family who were usually inspired by Christian charity to help others less fortunate than themselves. In many instances their resolve was strengthened by a desperate need to break out from the monotonous seclusion of life in a Victorian home; virtually every other avenue of employment was closed to them if they wished to remain members of society. Mostly, their activities were restricted to visiting the sick poor in their homes and supplying them with suitable comforts. Their nursing responsibilities rarely extended beyond soothing a fevered brow or smoothing a rumpled pillow—but in the days when nursing consisted of little more anyway, they had a valuable effect on morale. Florence Nightingale, however, deliberately excluded them from her Crimean party as she wanted only women who could give practical help. The second group of nurses, led by Mary Stanley, who left for the Crimea on December 2, 1854, was of a different fibre and did, as Sarah Anne tells us, contain Ladies.

In between the two extremes were the religious Orders, Roman Catholic and Anglican, of varying degrees of strictness. They learnt their nursing by experience, so their effectiveness depended on that experience. These Sisters of Mercy or of Charity (they were known by a variety of names) visited and nursed the sick—usually the sick poor—in their homes, but sometimes they brought the patient back to their convent. As Florence Nightingale noted[10] (again about those selected for service in military hospitals), 'Sisters of Mercy, as regards ward service, are decorous and kind, and sometimes inefficient and prudish'. Members of the Anglican Orders were mostly daughters of middle-class families whose motives were much the same as those of the Ladies.

A rather confusing feature of mid-19th century English medicine is the inter-relationship between nursing, hospitals, the home, and social class. Nobody rich or poor, went into hospital if they could possibly avoid it. So long as there was someone to look after them at home, patients were more comfortable, better treated, and certainly safer from the dangers of infection than they would be in hospital. The better-off could afford to employ nurses (of widely varying degrees of experience and ability) to help in caring for the sick person's needs. These nurses either lived-in or visited as circumstances demanded. The poor helped themselves, though they might be fortunate in scraping a penny or two together for a visit from a nurse with charitable feelings towards someone of her own kind. They might also hope for a call from a Sister of Mercy who was either seeking a convert or simply wishing to give practical comfort as in the case of Sarah Anne and her fellow Anglican Sellonites during the cholera epidemics in Plymouth.

Nevertheless the number of poor patients who received any sort of outside help was desperately small. They either died or got better naturally—though maybe with some lingering disability. But if they could not be cared for at home they would find themselves in hospital—or more likely the workhouse since at that time only about eight thousand hospital beds existed in the whole of England and Wales.

Nursing in the army was quite a different affair to nursing in civil life: it was self-contained and run on organized lines designed to meet military, rather than medical, needs. The nursing at this period was done by male orderlies who were either convalescent patients, pensioners, or soldiers temporarily posted by their commanding officers; thus for the most part they were a shifting, untrained population lacking any motivation. Military nursing was a necessary evil to be accomplished with as little disruption to military order as was possible. Practices did, nevertheless, vary in other countries, notably Roman Catholic ones, which helps to explain why the French were able to call on their Sisters of Charity for service in the Crimea.

In British eyes, the army was fully capable of looking after its own. There was no question of outside nursing assistance, and, in any case the quality of such assistance would, in most people's opinion, have made it a positive liability. Under the circumstances, Florence Nightingale's reception at Scutari was surprisingly favourable.

The stumbling block to nursing, both civilian and military, was its centuries-old position as a kind of domestic service—sometimes noble, but for long periods a hateful drudge. Strangely, perhaps, the fortunes of nursing were only loosely linked to those of medicine; the dominating influence was religion—and, as Sarah Anne makes so clear, this influence had in no way abated by the mid-19th century.

For the first fifteen hundred years of the Christian era, nursing had leant heavily on the monasteries. Unfortunately very little is known about nursing in monastic communities except that it was practised more with Christian charity than with a knowledge of medicine. But if proof is needed that nursing was a religious occupation it is given by the effects of the Reformation and the dissolution of the monasteries in the late 1530s in England.

The end of the monasteries marked the end of any passable system of nursing for the best part of three hundred years. Conditions deteriorated as callousness and even brutality entered the scene, and it was the sick poor who suffered most. The philanthropy of the rich no longer had a materially identifiable object, though ladies continued to visit the poor as they had been doing since Greek and Roman times. The few lay hospitals that were left could in no way meet the need, added to which their religious nursing Sisters were expelled, though the old monastic titles of Matron (in charge of the nurses) and Sister (in charge of the wards) were retained. In

England there was no such thing as a 'nursing class' and in consequence hospitals had to take what they could get—and that amounted to servants prepared to do unpleasant tasks in unpleasant surroundings. The Protestant Church was not imbued with the same sense of responsibility towards the sick as was the Catholic, and once nursing was dissociated from religion it lost its social standing.

Nursing was thus effectively destroyed and nothing was done to restore it. Women, in general, were subject to a masculine society, their education was neglected, and they were no longer permitted the freedom they had enjoyed in the past—the proper place for a respectable woman was in the home. The mere suggestion of a career was unthinkable. The propriety of nursing, even as Christian charity, had been forgotten. Women took up 'nursing' only when they saw no other way to survive.

The Continent did not suffer as badly at the Reformation as did England. The hospital system was stronger and the nursing Orders were determined to carry on—with varying degrees of success. However, there were abuses and to combat these the Sisters of Charity were, in 1633, born through the inspiration of the great social reformer, Vincent de Paul, and his devoted follower, Louise le Gras. The Sisters came from humble backgrounds all over France; they were subject to no vows or regulations since the institution was not religious in the monastic sense, though Vincent did emphasize that their calling was sacred. He appreciated that a monastic life with its religious observances was in conflict with the demands of nursing, particularly in people's homes. The Sisters of Charity passed through the Dark Age of nursing, from the 17th century to the middle of the 19th, like a shining light.

Never before this period nor since were conditions in civil hospitals so bad—open windows and ventilation were anathema; damp seeped in, walls were mildewed and fungous growth sprouted in corners; cockroaches and bugs flourished; the patients were filthy and crawling with vermin; dirt was everywhere and with it the germs of disease which spread feverishly from malnourished patient to malnourished patient. The 'nurses' were supposed to scrub and do the laundry, to empty spittoons, close-stools (commodes), and bedpans but without an adequate sanitary system effort was pointless. Nursing care just did not exist.

What is so difficult today is to gain some idea of the horror of hospital 'care' in those days and of how, when medicine itself was building its modern foundations, there could be such indifference to the plight of the sick poor. Thankfully, we have nothing in our own experience that gives us a yardstick, and so we have to accept that the worst we can imagine may well not approach the reality.

Reaction, when it came, was slow moving. The way was prepared by poor-law reform and by the developing revolution in public health and hygiene which began in the 1830s and continued for the best part of Queen Victoria's reign. The slums of industrial towns were festering sores where epidemics spread like wildfire; the morbidity and mortality rates throughout the country thoroughly alarmed the authorities and forced them into acting on the reports produced by the philanthropists.

The welfare of the individual sick person, however, took second place to the public health and despite scattered attempts to improve matters it took the Crimean War and the energy of Florence Nightingale to get nursing reform off the ground. Previous ventures were mostly overtly religious—if not to start with, they had become so. The early ones had been Roman Catholic and strongly influenced by the French model; for example, the Sisters of Mercy founded by Catherine McAuley. This Order was originally intended to give a home to destitute girls but in 1830 it concentrated on nursing; the Bermondsey branch, opened in 1839, provided five extremely able nuns for Florence Nightingale's party.

The first Protestant nursing order to appear in England was founded in 1840 by Mrs. Elizabeth Gurney Fry. It was known as the Protestant Sisters of Mercy or the Nursing Sisters, and for the first time training of a sort was given—though to say that it approached the Nightingale concept would be an overstatement; nevertheless it was a firm step in the right direction. The order was the first to be approached by Florence Nightingale when forming her party for Scutari, but the Lady Superintendent refused to comply with the conditions laid down by the Government.

In 1845 the Park Village Community (whose members were also known as Sisters of Mercy) was founded by the Rev. Edward Pusey's High Church movement. This was followed in 1848 by the Sellonite Sisters of Mercy and by St. John's House, Westminster, another High Church sisterhood which sent six of its members with the Nightingale party. Others including the Protestant Institution for Nurses in Devonshire Square—they refused to allow any of their members to work outside their own control—were formed soon after. The thin end of the wedge had thus been inserted into Victorian society: nursing was on the verge of becoming respectable, even though it was still regarded more as an act of charity and religious devotion than as the physical care of a sick body. Moreover, despite these nursing orders being sponsored by the Church of England there was a constant suspicion that they were sailing under false colours—a suspicion that in many cases, both individual and collective, proved to be true. The Catholic tradition in nursing was strong.

So, when public opinion demanded that nurses be sent to the Crimea the nation found that it did possess a varied assortment to choose from, but mostly they were women living an other-worldly existence doing work that ill-prepared them for the real task of nursing they would meet at Scutari. Their response, nevertheless, was immediate:

'Many was the band that was that week organized for the work; many were the individuals who in their secluded homes determined to offer their services for this purpose, and applied for information and permission to the official authorities.'[11] But it was a fluttering movement lacking direction and leadership. Had these Sisters and Lady Volunteers ventured as such to the Crimea, they would have received short shrift from the military and been packed off home on the next boat. What was missing was an administrative genius capable of welding a motley collection of women into an effective unit with a single purpose—a leader with strength enough to subdue their religious fervour and differences, to control the behaviour of the professional nurses, and with influence in high places to ride through governmental red tape. The genius *was* there, standing in the wings, well rehearsed, and simply awaiting her cue.

By any standard Florence Nightingale was a remarkable woman and Sarah Anne's immediate assessment of her qualities at their first meeting goes a long way towards explaining the 34-year-old Miss Nightingale's assured command of both people and events. She moved in the upper reaches of Victorian society, travelling extensively on the Continent and numbering among her friends Elizabeth Barrett Browning, George Eliot, Lord Shaftesbury, Lord Palmerston, and Sidney Herbert (whom she first met in Rome in 1847). Yet for ten years she had been struggling to free herself from the entangling web of that society. For ten years she had known that her purpose in life was to reform nursing and to ensure that those who nursed were properly trained for the responsibility. For ten years, despite strong family disapproval and social disbelief, she had prepared herself for the moment when the world would listen to her—the moment that came with the calamity of the Crimea. She visited hospitals and nursing Orders on the Continent, studying their administration, watching operations, all the while compulsively taking notes and drawing comparisons. She obtained a multitude of public health and hospital reports, and filled notebook after notebook with comment and observation; she was sent private reports on hospitals from friends in Paris and Berlin; eventually, thanks largely to her social connections, she was recognized for what she had made herself: the leading expert on hospitals and sanitary conditions in

Setting the Scene

Europe. Then in the spring of 1854 she began to visit hospitals in England with the express purpose of gathering ammunition for her campaign to reform the terrible working conditions of nurses. In this she had the unqualified support of Sidney Herbert who was himself seeking reliable information about the bad pay and worse lodging of nurses in an attempt to focus public opinion on the evils. Both were fighting an uphill battle as public opinion accepted the *status quo* and in any event could not see how change could come about.

But then came Russell's despatches. After the first, describing the plight of the wounded after the battle of the Alma on September 20, which was published in *The Times* on October 9, Florence Nightingale acted. She gathered a small party of about half-a-dozen professional nurses and, with herself in charge, was prepared to sail on the 17th. On the 12th she had seen Lord Palmerston who had given her expedition his approval. On the 13th she had visited Dr. Andrew Smith who, in his usual rough manner, had informed her that all was well in Scutari and, in answer to her question about what she should take with her, had assured her that nothing was needed. He did, however, give her a letter of introduction to Dr. Menzies, the medical superintendent at the Scutari General Hospital.

But, on the 15th Sidney Herbert wrote to her officially asking her to take a party out to Scutari. This put an entirely different complexion on the matter, particularly as Mr. Herbert suggested increasing the number of nurses to at least 40. The old plan was scrapped, but as Florence Nightingale wanted to leave within a week, the new party had to be assembled without delay. A headquarters was therefore established at the Herberts' London home at 49 Belgrave Square. Here, a committee consisting of Miss Mary Stanley (sister of Arthur Stanley, Dean of Westminster), Mrs. Charles Bracebridge, Lady Canning and Lady Cranworth began to interview applicants—a task that slowly dampened their original enthusiasm. Out of some sixty or seventy hopefuls only eleven were considered to have had sufficient experience of nursing in hospital and even they were

27

not of the best calibre—only one gave a reason other than money for wanting to be included in the party. The number of these professional nurses was made up to fourteen by the addition of three from the aborted expedition.

The uniforms issued to these nurses were hastily made and mostly fitted where they touched. They were also hideously unattractive, consisting of a grey tweed dress, a grey worsted jacket, a short woollen cloak, and a white cap. Round the shoulders a holland scarf was worn with the words 'Scutari Hospital' embroidered on it in red. This uniform did, however, succeed in its primary objective which was to identify the wearer as a nurse and so save her from the unwelcome attentions of the troops. The nuns and Sisters in the party were spared the charade and were allowed to wear their own habit or uniform dress.

While the committee was sifting the professionals, Florence Nightingale was going the rounds of the institutions and communities in London. From these she collected ten Roman Catholic nuns (five from the convent in Bermondsey and five from the orphanage in Norwood) and six Sisters from St. John's House—although the Master took two days to agree to Miss Nightingale's terms. Towards the middle of the week Miss Sellon came forward with the offer of some of her own Sisters and the services of eight were accepted even though this meant sending to Devon for Sarah Anne and three others. The party was completed by Selina Bracebridge, who was in charge of the domestic side, and by Charles, her husband, who saw to the financial and travelling arrangements. Florence Nightingale herself was in charge and on the 19th she received formal Cabinet confirmation of her appointment as Superintendent of the Female Nursing Establishment of the English General Hospitals in Turkey. This grandiose title makes it plain that she was going to Scutari not as a practising nurse but, as she wished, as an administrator. The Commander in the Field, Lord Raglan, was informed of her impending arrival as was Dr. John Hall and the Purveyor-in-Chief. Dr. Smith wrote personally to Menzies with instructions that every help should be afforded to Miss Nightingale and her nurses. It was the Director General's wish that the medical officers 'should use every endeavour to render the nurses useful in their position'.[12]

Although Sidney Herbert believed that there were sufficient doctors and supplies at Scutari, he was uneasy about the reports he was receiving and he warned Florence Nightingale that he was immediately sending out a commission to look into the state of the hospitals and the condition of the sick and wounded. This was the Hospitals Commission—made up of Benson Maxwell, a barrister, and Drs. Cumming and Laing. The purpose of the Commission was solely to establish the facts, not to take any action.

After the Nightingale party had left for Scutari, Mary Stanley continued to recruit—but with an ulterior motive. In the privacy of her heart she had become a Roman Catholic (she made this public knowledge when she was received into the Catholic church in the spring of 1855) and, probably out of jealousy, she wished to establish Catholic dominance in the Turkish hospitals. By sheer determination and the force of her personality, Florence Nightingale had succeeded in getting together a group of women who agreed to abide by her orders in all matters relating to the hospital, to attend primarily to the bodily needs of their patients, and never to introduce religious subjects except with patients of their own faith. Mary Stanley's venture came close to wrecking all this.

The Stanley party, which arrived in Scutari on December 15, consisted of 15 Roman Catholic nuns, 9 Lady Volunteers, and 22 nurses. The nuns recognized the authority only of their Mother Superior and were chiefly concerned with gaining souls. The Ladies, for the most part, resented having to perform menial tasks and believed that they should be waited on by the nurses. And the professional nurses were representative of the worst of their kind—drunken, coarse, promiscuous, and useless.

The religious dissension stirred up by these new arrivals in what had hitherto been an atmosphere of almost miraculous harmony was quite shameful, though Sarah Anne did her best to look on the bright side and seek out the redeeming features. For Florence Nightingale, though, already facing a challenge to her authority over the Sister Wheeler affair (which Sarah Anne describes in her journal) and coping with a medical disaster that had still to reach its height, this new disruptive influence could well have been the breaking point. But her courage and determination brought her triumphantly through.

Although women continued to come out to the Crimean theatre, the original party with Sarah Anne and the other Sellonites were the only nurses to work through the whole winter and to see order brought out of the most appalling chaos. They were something very special—and Florence Nightingale realized this. 'Our own old party,' she wrote to her sister, 'which began its work in hardship, toil, struggle and obscurity has done better than any other ... The small beginning, the simple hardship, the silent and *gradual* struggle upwards; these are the climate in which an enterprise really thrives and grows.'[13]

THE SELLONITES

Sarah Anne was indeed fortunate in her choice of nursing Order and in joining during its early days for Miss Priscilla Lydia Sellon trained her Sisters well—maybe not in the skills of nursing for these were to be learnt by experience, but in true Christian charity. She taught them courtesy and good manners, not to talk down to those they were helping and to be understanding of their shortcomings. They were always to act as if everyone was honest and spoke the truth. They were never to shrink from dirt or be shocked at physical deformity. To the sick, the destitute, or the orphaned they were always to be gentle, kind, considerate, and indulgent and perhaps most valuable of all they were trained to keep their presence of mind whatever the circumstance. As the first of the Sisters lived up to these high standards, it is small wonder that Florence Nightingale readily accepted Miss Sellon's offer of help and that the Sellonites who went to the Crimea proved their mettle.

Priscilla Sellon had come to Stoke, an area of Devonport, in 1847, and here she took cheap lodgings. She was, as Margaret Goodman expressed it, 'deeply moved by the wretchedness of many of the poor, especially in maritime towns . . . [and] determined to devote her little fortune, together with what other talents God had committed to her, to the relief of misery'.[14]

News of her intentions spread and before long she had gathered around her a number of other ladies including Sarah Anne Terrot. From the start the religious inclinations (Anglican) were evident: the three large houses acquired by the Sisterhood in the slums of Plymouth were known as the 'Abbey' and the Sisters who worked from there were the 'Order of the Holy Communion'. Their dress sufficiently resembled that of a Sister of Mercy to make them immediately recognizable, and as such they were able to move through the worst parts of the town at any hour without let or hindrance.

The Bishop of Exeter took a warm interest in the new Sisterhood; he appreciated that it could perform an extremely valuable and much needed service in the community, but he was anxious lest it should prove merely a cover for Catholic infiltration or that Catholic influence would pervert active, useful nurses into ascetic recluses. He warned against submission to Holy Obedience, as such vows were only fetters that bound to spiritual slavery, and he objected to the way the Sisters were cut off from their families—though, as Margaret Goodman observed: if medical men and even hired nurses never allowed themselves to fear contagion, how much less did Sisters of Mercy as they were alone in the world, with none dependent on them and leaving no gap in a family circle should the worst befall them.[15]

So, with the Bishop's counsel, the Sellonites made an excellent beginning. In the cholera epidemics of 1849 and 1852 they nursed the patients in their homes and opened a special hospital for the worst cases. Orphans of the epidemics were taken in and cared for. The only rule at their foundation came from St. John, chapter 15, verses 12–14: 'This is my commandment, That ye love one another, as I have loved you. Greater love hath no man than this, that a man lay down his life for his friends. Ye are my friends, if ye do whatsoever I command you.' They were happy.

The chief concern of the Sisters was to minister to the temporal needs of the sick and the wretched—and they interpreted this in the broadest possible manner. In fact, at the beginning Miss Sellon was even accused of being too secular in her work. There was a school-room in the 'Abbey' primarily intended for the orphans who lived there, but open to outsiders as well. A reading room was available on two evenings a week and the Sisters would help with the education in subjects such as French and drawing of anyone who asked. Spare rooms in the 'Abbey' were let to people who agreed to abide by a few simple regulations. And in the winter months at noon on Wednesdays and Fridays any elderly person whose working days were past could come in for a dinner of soup and a piece of bread.

To acquire a base in London the Sisterhood amalgamated with the St. Saviour's Sisterhood; but the union was not altogether a success as the Sellonites were regarded as being too Protestant—by 1863 more than half the women who had at some time been associated with St. Saviour's had joined the Church of Rome.[16] The building of the new headquarters of the combined Sisterhood was delightfully described by Margaret Goodman:

'The first conventual edifice was erected for the Sisterhood in Osnaburg Street; where building operations were for some time suspended, because Government was not able to decide whether religious houses were in accordance with the genius of the English law: ultimately, however, the Legislature suffered the work to proceed.'[17]

Unfortunately, Miss Sellon's original conception was too good, too naive, to survive untouched in those days of cut-throat proseletyzing. The Tractarians[18] interfered with the Sisterhood to such an extent that they eventually succeeded in destroying all that it stood for; their influence, already apparent before the Crimea, really gathered momentum after the war.

A closed branch of the Sisterhood, the 'Order of the Sacred Heart' was formed at the Priory at Bradford in Wiltshire (later it moved to Ascot Heath). Life there was extremely conventual and the Sisters most devout. But even the open Order with its branches in Plymouth and London became absorbed with spiritual concerns. The original guiding rule became overlaid by a host of petty laws; for instance, at first the only restriction on conversation was talking shop during recreation, but later just about every natural subject was tabooed which left, as Margaret Goodman put it, only the cat and the weather. The end result was a rule of almost perpetual silence for both Orders.

The Sisters grew callous towards each other—though they remained kind to the poor. The Plymouth branch under Miss Sellon in particular 'suffered from want of the commonest care . . . It was a fault even to do anything for a sick person without the "Mother's" orders; and she, late at night, late in the morning, unpunctual at all times, would forget to give any'.[19] Margaret Goodman believed that although Miss Sellon claimed supreme authority she was probably ignorant of the true state of affairs in the Sisterhood. And by 1863 the entire institution, unchecked by Episcopal supervision, had 'become almost valueless, even as a source of charity'.[20]

THE ARMY DOCTORS AND THEIR HOSPITALS

Since Sarah Anne's prime concern was for the soldiers as individuals, she does not fill in the background to the disasters at Scutari—it would probably have been incomprehensible to her anyway. Nevertheless, she most astutely pin-pointed the essential facts: on her arrival the men in the wards were suffering from the effects of cold, fatigue, exposure, bowel diseases, and malnutrition—and many of these soldiers had never even reached the Crimea. Then, after she had been at Scutari for only a fortnight she could write that, although the hospitals were gradually improving, the state of the men coming into them was growing steadily worse. And, finally, she commented on the inferior quality of the hospital orderlies. Disease was nothing new to the army, so why were the pressures on the hospitals not anticipated by the medical administration?

The answers lie in Lord Raglan's management of his troops and of their medical support which precipitated the situation and in the out-of-date medical organization that had to deal with the consequences. Moreover, the fact that the Army Medical Department was, as it had always been, a civilian department did not improve matters, as it and its staff were devoid of military authority. (Not until 1898 did the Department become the Royal Army Medical Corps with officers and men having substantive military rank.) Its administration, too, was hopeless: when the Department had come into being with the creation of the Standing Army in 1660, it was separated into two branches, staff and regimental, each working within its own special compartment, each with its own sphere of responsibilities with the result that the seeds of administrative chaos were present from the very start. Nevertheless, at its origin the system did what was required of it passably well, but by the middle of Queen Victoria's reign it was suffering from severe hardening of the arteries. An example of this is Staff Surgeon First Class Duncan Menzies' predicament.

When, in April 1854, the British army was gathering at Scutari there was no thought of establishing a military general hospital[21] (a staff responsibility). The regimental surgeons simply moved into the large Turkish military hospital (by agreement) where each ran his own regimental hospital with Menzies acting as the co-ordinating staff officer. At the end of

April, Menzies realized that the formation of a general hospital would be inevitable so he wrote to the Director General asking for the regulations governing general hospitals. Dr. Smith, in London, replied that there were none. As he wrote later:

'The untoward position in which I found myself, led me immediately to require the records of the Department to be searched, in the hope that they might, by supplying information in reference to the events which were observed, and the wants that arose during the campaign in Spain and Portugal, afford what under existing circumstances was so greatly needed. The search however proved unproductive, as only two or three valueless documents were found.'[22]

To have no regulations or orders to follow—not even ones applicable to the Peninsular War—was a catastrophe in itself. Small wonder then that, when the regimental hospitals moved out of the building in early June and Menzies became the medical superintendent of what had suddenly become a general hospital, he followed so far as he could the only rules available to him—those for regimental hospitals.[23] However, the administration and the functions of the two styles of hospital varied considerably. In consequence, people were playing one game according to the rules of another, and if someone chose to be bloody-minded (as usually happened) he could obstruct the whole field of play. The situation at Scutari and the trials and tribulations Sarah Anne had to endure can thus be better understood if we know a little about the various rules and how they came into existence.

But first, a fundamental aspect of the military mind should be appreciated. War is a game full of complex rituals, played according to certain well-defined rules, and any change is vigorously resisted. This attitude was acceptable when war was a small, almost tribal, affair, but it was responsible for many catastrophic incidents (of which the Crimea is one of the best known) when war outgrew its childhood. Part and parcel of the attitude was the view that the military machine was all-powerful and that anything that interrupted play was a nuisance—and among the greatest nuisances were the sick and wounded, together with those who tried to help them. The French military surgeon, Pierre François Percy, for instance, was driven to remark in 1799: 'What administration! To see the indifference, the lethargy of all those at the head of affairs. When one speaks to them about the hospitals, one would believe that the sick and wounded cease to be men when they can no longer be soldiers.'[24] It was a state of mind that knew no frontiers. Indeed, with few exceptions, such as the Roman army and the British army under Marlborough, the value to an army's morale of a good medical service passed unappreciated throughout history until the 20th century—the concept of morale was in any case ill-formed.

The Army Medical Department, under its Director General, had absolute control over its staff officers, but was responsible for the regimental surgeons only insofar as their professional standards and conduct were concerned. For the rest, these surgeons were entirely under the military discipline of their commanding officers; they, in fact, held commissions in their regiments and wore the regimental uniform.

The staff medical officers were inspector generals, deputy inspector generals, and staff surgeons;[25] their duties were a mixture of the administrative (particularly in the senior two ranks) and the medical. The staff surgeons usually served in garrison or general hospitals, but when in the field they were employed at brigade, or sometimes divisional, level. Like the Department itself, staff officers were all civilians, though in 1841 the staff surgeon first class had been given the equivalent rank of major and the staff surgeon second class that of captain —but this was an empty gesture on the part of the Commander-in-Chief as the ranks still carried no military authority. A staff surgeon might be superintendent of a hospital but he had to have a field officer (who might be of lower rank) in overall command to maintain discipline. Assisting the staff surgeons in hospitals were staff assistant surgeons.

However, the heart of the army's medical organization was

the regimental surgeon who, at the time of the Crimea, had two regimental assistant surgeons under him. Medically the regiment looked after its own; it carried with it the paraphernalia for setting up a regimental hospital, including a marquee for occasions when no suitable building could be found, beds, bedding, ward utensils such as urinals and bed pans, dressings, and a large chest containing six months' supply of medicines. Transport for all this was a regimental responsibility. For the sake of convenience and mutual support a number of regimental hospitals would sometimes come together as a brigade hospital, as happened at Scutari before the army moved on to Varna.

Regulations governing regimental hospitals began to appear around 1770. Most dealt with matters of conduct, rations, and pay while a soldier was ill, but one was to be the cause of considerable misery at Scutari: every man had to bring with him into the hospital his knapsack containing a clean shirt, a hairbrush and comb, eating utensils, and other necessaries. The disregard for the realities of warfare was sublime. Admittedly there was provision for clothing, and anything else the sick man might require, to be properly brought in, but this had no relevance whatsoever in the Crimean situation. On arrival at Scutari, virtually no one had a knapsack (they had been abandoned on Lord Raglan's orders when the army landed in the Crimea) but as the regulations decreed that they had, in the eyes of authority they all had, and there were no rules whereby the deficiencies could be made good.

The staffing of the regimental hospitals was again a regimental concern; medical orderlies and non-medical personnel such as cooks, ward-masters, storemen, office staff, and so forth were detailed by the commanding officer and the band provided the stretcher bearers. Soldiers' wives who followed the regiment were at first encouraged to undertake nursing duties and to do the cooking and washing, but gradually they were edged out until in 1832 they were no longer employed in any capacity. Although none of the soldier orderlies had special training, the system worked reasonably well (by 18th-century standards); indeed many orderlies had long experience and performed their tasks admirably. Convalescent patients also helped, though Florence Nightingale had something to say about this:

'It is often said,' she wrote, 'that, in regimental hospitals, patients ought to "nurse each other", because the number of sick altogether being, say, but thirty, and out of these one only perhaps being seriously ill, and the other twenty-nine having little the matter with them, and nothing to do, they should be set to nurse the one; also, that soldiers are so trained to obey, that they will be the most obedient, and therefore the best of nurses, add to which they are always kind to their comrades.

'Now, have those who say this, considered that, in order to obey, you must know *how* to obey, and that these soldiers certainly do not know how to obey in nursing. I have seen these "kind" fellows (and how kind they are no one knows so well as myself) move a comrade so that, in one case at least, the man died in the act.'[26]

These remarks were, in fact, her tactful way of drawing attention to one of the serious defects in the system; the lack of training of *all* those who nursed the sick and wounded.

One other rule, which was workable so long as the system continued to function as the administration intended but was the cause of friction at Scutari, concerned food and its payment. When a soldier was a patient in his regimental hospital, his basic ration was drawn by his Company; other items he might need were bought by the hospital sergeant out of stoppages levied on the patient's pay.

Thus, during peacetime the regimental hospital system could fulfil its obligations which amounted to being self-contained and not bothering anyone else. But during a war, the situation changed, a fact that was appreciated, however reluctantly, by the authorities who formed general hospitals to accompany the army overseas to give support after battle and to hold the long-term sick when the regiment was on the move

—they were established in existing hospitals or, in the early period, in large buildings.

In 1690 when staff hospitals first appeared they were of two sorts: the fixed hospital which developed into the general hospital, and the marching hospital which developed into the flying hospital. The marching hospital was, as its name implies, reasonably mobile and had its own tentage and transport waggons. Its function was to act as a casualty clearing station between the regimental hospital and the fixed hospital; it was an invaluable part of the system since it meant that there were clear administrative and transport links between front and rear. Flying hospitals were, however, perversely done away with during the Peninsular War (their transport waggons cluttered the roads); instead, the staff surgeon who was acting as senior medical officer to the brigade had to apply to the Commissary General for transport to evacuate the sick and wounded. The consequence, so far as the Crimean War was concerned, was a great administrative divide between the regiments at the front and the general hospital at Scutari.

The general hospital, which today is an indispensable part of casualty evacuation and treatment, has had an extremely chequered career; in fact, so many have been the low points that it is impossible to choose the lowest, but certainly the state at the beginning of the Crimean campaign is a strong contender. In contrast to the regimental hospitals, general hospitals were unpopular with all concerned: with the casualties because they were removed from friends and a familiar environment; with commanding officers because the men were lost to them for an excessive length of time; and with many senior doctors for a variety of reasons, both administrative and medical. But overshadowing all these reasons was the terrible fear of infection; even in those days it was known that when men were crowded together infectious diseases spread like wildfire and a particularly vicious form of wound infection known as hospital gangrene was an ever-present menace. This was nothing either new or peculiar to British military hospitals;

during Napoleon's campaign of 1813, the hospitals from Dresden to the Rhine and beyond were quite justifiably called the sepulchres of the Grande Armée.[27]

In wartime general hospitals were accepted as a necessary evil but in peacetime their number was reduced to absurd levels. Indeed for a long while no arrangements were made in Britain for dealing with the sick returning from overseas. The Transport Commissioners were responsible for them so long as they were being transported, but what happened to them after they were landed was no one's concern. Their plight was pitiful and a shame to the country. Relief of a sort came only in 1781 when the first general military hospital was opened in England. Nevertheless between 1802 and 1806 the general hospitals at Gosport, Plymouth, and Deal had been closed by the surgical member of the Army Medical Board on grounds of economy—when it was found that it cost 17d a day to keep a man in a general hospital, but only 10d in a regimental hospital, the fate of the general hospital was sealed.

So, in 1809 some 6,000 sick and wounded arrived in Portsmouth from Corunna to find not a single hospital ready for them. Only the prompt improvisation of Dr. James McGrigor, the local inspector of hospitals, saved the situation from complete disaster, but even so probably a thousand men died unnecessarily before the three general hospitals were re-opened. Then in the years of peace after Waterloo the Government turned the economic screw and the Army Medical Department was squeezed to the bone. General hospitals were cut back again so that apart from two of minor importance, there was only Fort Pitt at Chatham to cater for the troops invalided home from garrisons overseas. McGrigor, who became Director General in 1815 and held the post until 1851 (he was knighted in 1831), was not unduly upset by this, despite his previous experience, since he was a staunch believer in the regimental system. The net result was that by the time war was declared in the Crimea, no general hospital had been established for forty years and indeed any thought that one might be needed—certainly in Europe—had been regarded as faintly ridiculous.

Female nurses had been employed in military general hospitals until the early 19th century and had featured prominently in all major campaigns. However, the provision of other subordinate staff such as medical orderlies, cooks, clerks, and all remaining non-medical personnel fell to the lot of the units in the field—and this was a disaster. Not surprisingly, human nature being what it is, the commanding officers seized on the opportunity to off-load their more difficult and undesirable characters with the result that ill-discipline, drunkenness, and thieving were the rule. Admittedly attempts had been made during and after the Peninsular War to introduce a Veterans' Battalion to act as hospital orderlies and stretcher bearers, but with a notable lack of success. They were untrained and too feeble or crippled to carry out the work expected of them; they also had a fondness for the bottle.

The administration of the few general hospitals that did exist was in little better state and did nothing to enhance their reputation. The military commandants could be posted elsewhere at a moment's notice, so there was lack of continuity at the top. Added to this they disliked the job and were invariably ignorant of hospital organization and administration, so there was also inefficiency and lack of enthusiasm. The absence of a firm administrative hand was sorely felt at Scutari. Nevertheless, so far as the hospital inmates were concerned, the greatest deficiencies were in food, clothing, medicines, and dressings, the responsibilities of the purveyors and apothecaries.

The purveyors' original task had been to distribute food to the sick and wounded, but they soon gained responsibility for contracting for supplies and for cooking the food. Later, in 1795, they were given the jobs of finding accommodation for the hospital and of providing beds, bedding, ward furniture, and lighting. Theirs, too, was the responsibility of finding subordinate staff either by requesting headquarters to detail men from the regiments or by recruiting them from civilian sources.

Purveyors were at first drawn from staff and regimental surgeons, but with the start of the Peninsular War this practice
ceased as qualified men were in short supply and urgently
needed for medical duties; the purveyors' clerks became the purveyors. During this war they became responsible for the arms,
accoutrements, clothing, and other necessaries of the patients;
the rations, medical comforts, and other stores they obtained
through the Commissariat Department—or if this proved
impracticable, by local requisitioning. The cost of items the
patients needed in hospital was paid to the Medical Department by the regiment from stoppages in the soldiers' pay.

Later, after the war, most of the stores had to be obtained
by the Ordnance Department before being transferred to the
purveyor. But the next event was to have the most profound
repercussions at Scutari: the Accountant's Branch of the
Medical Department was closed for reasons of economy and
its responsibilities taken over by the Secretary at War. As a
result the purveyors thought that they were now answerable
to the War Office and not to the Director General. So, when
Dr. Menzies was trying to establish a general hospital at Scutari he could get no co-operation from the purveyor (whose
responsibilities in this respect were enormous, both as regards
finance and supplies); Mr. Ward said that he either made
decisions on his own or referred matters to the War Office.

But hospital duties were not the end of the purveyor's
responsibilities. In 1827, McGrigor, the then Director General,
laid down that during the evacuation of casualties the purveyor
was responsible for the hospital equipment carried on transport ships, and also for the cleanliness, ventilation, and general
equipping of the vessels. When the casualties were landed, he
had a duty to see that medical comforts, supplies of food, and
cooking utensils were carried on the waggons and that stretcher
bearers were available to carry the wounded into hospital.
Yet three years later, such was the run-down of the Army
Medical Department that the office of purveyor had become
obsolete.

Consequently in 1854 veterans of the Peninsular War had to be brought out of retirement to perform a most formidable and demanding job, the existence of which, officially at any rate, was in limbo. Hence the elderly Mr. Ward at Scutari and hence an explanation for the inflexibility in the hospital management. The diet rolls, mentioned by Sarah Anne, were an example of this inflexibility in operation. She does not describe them in detail, but Frances Taylor, a lady volunteer who went out with Mary Stanley's party, did so:

'First, the diet roll. In London hospitals a diet card for each patients hangs at the head of his bed, and any alteration in it is generally, if not always, made by the house-surgeon. In military hospitals the diet roll is a book of foolscap paper, with a sheet for each day, and small divisions for each diet. Whatever is inserted in the diet rolls (as in all hospitals), cannot be furnished till the next day. In military hospitals a man is placed either on full, half, low, or spoon diet. If a man is on full diet, one column is sufficient, as by it is understood that he is to have daily 1lb. of meat, ditto of bread, ditto of potatoes, and two pints of tea, also half-a-pint of porter. Half-diet is exactly half of this. Low-diet the half again of that. Spoon-diet is simply one pound of bread and two pints of tea; but it has this difference, that the surgeon may give a man on spoon-diet extras; but for any patients on full, half, or low diet he may not: nor may the surgeons order more than two or three extras to the spoon-diets—the extras at this time were fowls, mutton chops, potatoes, milk, eggs, arrowroot, rice, sago, and lemons for lemonade.

'Before the diet roll could be sent into the purveyor's stores it had to be signed by the assistant-surgeon in charge of the patients, whose names were inserted on it, and then it had to be countersigned by the staff-surgeon of the division. The staff-surgeon being the assistant-surgeon's superior officer, and medical etiquette entirely sinking in military discipline, it is quite possible that an assistant-surgeon may be called to account for any extravagance in the diet roll, and this sometimes happened, for extravagance seemed to be the great bugbear of our Eastern hospitals.

'The diet rolls were written by the sergeants or corporals appointed as ward masters; if they made any mistake (which they very often did) there was no redress. If they had forgotten to insert an extra to such a name, he must for that day go without it.

'The purveying department was at that time in a most inefficient state; constantly the requirements of the diet rolls were not complied with, the stores were given out most irregularly, the orderlies were often obliged to go down to the store-rooms at four A.M. to draw the rations for breakfast; the last of the band would not be served till past seven A.M. The men's dinners, which ought to have come at twelve, often did not come till five or six P.M.—three P.M. was thought excellent time. Very often we saw the orderlies cutting up the carcasses of sheep in the corridor close by the beds in which were men suffering from every form of disease.

'Of course many cases must arise in which the patients are in such a state that their diet must be altered or added to that day. The means of doing this is by a requisition signed by the assistant-surgeon. He must write a separate requisition for each man, and after he has signed it, it is taken to the staff-surgeon to be countersigned, and then to the stores.

'This regulation, and indeed all others, were made for military hospitals in an ordinary state, when the buildings only hold the numbers they are intended for, where every department is sufficiently supplied with people to work it, where extreme cases are to be counted in each ward by ones and twos, and can then of course receive the full attention of the surgeon; but these same laws brought to bear in the Eastern hospitals in that unprecedented time of distress became useless—extreme cases in Scutari were counted by one or two hundreds—it was a matter of impossibility for surgeons to write requisitions enough for their patients' wants, especially as they had to be countersigned by the staff-surgeon, a man having a large charge besides many other duties, and who was never sure of being found in any one place after the regular hours of going his rounds. The purveying department was also so utterly inefficient that constantly requisitions were signed and sent in, and then not honoured.'[28]

The apothecaries, as the name indicates, had charge of the medicines, dressings, and instruments in a general hospital; and, like the hospital itself, they faded away after Waterloo until in 1830 they were no longer needed. The Army Medical Department became responsible for assessing the quantity of drugs and dressings required and from 1842 had obtained half the supply from the Society of Apothecaries in London and half from two commercial firms—an arrangement that worked perfectly satisfactorily. However, in October 1854 the appointment was resurrected and qualified medical officers were given the equivalent rank of lieutenant. The apothecary appointed to Scutari was Dr. Reade, and when he died on November 25 of the same year, it was found that he had kept no accounts or records.

Finally, adding to all these fertile sources of inefficiency was the telegraph. Previously, once an expedition with its equipment and surgical staff for a general hospital had left England, its principal medical officer took full administrative control—no other course was possible—and replacement medical officers and supplies were despatched on request or as London felt was necessary. But thanks to the telegraph the Crimea was no longer remote; the Director General retained command of a medical service whose reported misfortunes left him utterly bewildered. The seeds of administrative chaos, germinating over many years, certainly came into full flower in the first winter of the Crimean War.

The staffing, equipping, and supplying of the hospitals at Scutari was the Department's responsibility, but there was a world of difference between Smith giving orders and making requisitions in London, and what actually came to pass at the other end. We shall come back to these problems later, but first a word or two amplifying Sarah Anne's description of the hospital buildings at Scutari will help us to understand some of the problems facing both doctors and nurses. In a nutshell these were the vast size of the buildings (despite which they became desperately overcrowded), their appalling latrines, and the dilapidation and unsuitability of the barracks for use as a hospital.

The General Hospital where Sarah Anne worked from the beginning of December had originally been a Turkish military hospital and, with one formidable drawback, not too bad a one at that: spacious and well ventilated, with an adequate water supply, bathing facilities, and stoves in the wards. There were beds for six hundred and sixty patients in the wards with perfectly adequate overflow accommodation for another four hundred and twenty six in the corridors. The drawback was the nature of the latrines; these were of the Turkish squatting variety with drains discharging straight into the sea and with no intervening water traps and no flushing system. There was nothing to stop the smell wafting back into the wards and an on-shore breeze was distinctly unwelcome. Since 'polluted air' was believed to be responsible for the transmission of disease, the soldiers threw any rubbish they could find into the drains in the vain hope of blocking the stink. Fatigue parties were ordered to clear the mess but they fought a losing battle. The engineers were called in to help, but they could do nothing to improve matters since the drains were deeply embedded in the fabric of the building. Only in the spring of 1855 after the Sanitary Commission had arrived were new flush lavatories installed and the sewage outflows water-trapped.

Another disturbing feature of the hospital environment was the closeness of the burial grounds. Apart from the demoralizing effect of this, the Turks buried the dead neither deeply nor securely with the result that still more noxious odours drifted into the hospital when the wind was in the south.

The Barrack Hospital where Sarah Anne and the rest of the Nightingale party were accommodated on their arrival was a different story. The Sultan Seline Barracks had been built as barracks and were commandeered as a depot when the British army began to concentrate at Scutari for the forthcoming campaign. They were taken over as a (general) hospital in September 1854 with Staff Surgeon First Class McGrigor (no relation to Sir James McGrigor) as superintendent—but once a barracks, always a barracks unless expensive modifications are undertaken. The building was immense, on two and three floors set around a central parade ground. It would have been a hospital administrator's nightmare in the best of circumstances. Parts of it were in a shocking state of disrepair; the latrines were of the same style as those in the General Hospital but with worse problems as, after heavy rain, they were prone to flood back into the wards. Men in the last stages of bowel diseases had neither the will nor the inclination to paddle across the floor through an inch of sewage to reach the latrine, so they did not. The water supply was sufficient in quantity but was not laid on in the wards and could only be drawn at two or three places—on one occasion the water was found to be filtering through the carcase of a horse. And there was no operating theatre, for which reason the hospital was originally intended only for the sick—when wounded in need of surgery began arriving, they were operated on where they lay in the wards and corridors.

The parts of the building that were usable from the start gave adequate space for about one thousand and sixty five beds in both wards and the inner corridors that overlooked the parade ground. However, the beds in the wards were Turkish divans—low wooden shelves set around the walls. Besides complicating the problems of nursing, these were extremely difficult to clean and harboured rats. When, in November 1854, the sick and wounded descended in a flood on Scutari, Menzies was compelled to open the dilapidated parts of the buildings as well.

Although the barracks had become a hospital, they still retained some of the functions of a depot. Reinforcements on their way to the Crimea were quartered there, and the wives and children left behind lived in some of the rooms in squalid, filthy conditions—as Sarah Anne soon discovered. These women and soldiers heaped yet more problems on Menzies' plate as they were usually drunk and noisy and could not be kept from the wards.

Mercifully, though, the departing regiments had left behind more than a hundred sick in the General Hospital with orderlies, cooks, store-keepers, and others to look after them. Although these men formed the nucleus of Menzies' subordinate staff, the blessing was decidedly mixed since the regiments had inevitably left their worst behind. The military commandant of the hospital was a Major Sillery (the same rank as Staff Surgeon First Class Menzies) who was not renowned for the exercise of initiative when the going grew tough.

Estimates of the number of casualties in the Crimea vary widely, nevertheless the figures given by Cantlie[29] for the month of January 1855 indicate the size of the medical disaster when it was at its height. Out of an army of 30,000 men, 11,328 were admitted to hospital; of these 3,168 died. These figures include only 119 wounded. On average 26.8 per cent of the army's strength was sick during each month of that winter; the next year between October 1855 and March 1856 it was 3.6 per cent which was lower than the rate for troops in the United Kindom. By the spring of 1855 Scutari had been transformed and the death rate had fallen from the 36 per cent level of January to 5.2 per cent in May.

Dramatic though these figures are, they do not reveal the full extent of Florence Nightingale's accomplishment: this comes in a comparison with the medical services of the other armies and what they managed to achieve. As Miss Nightingale herself described these services[30] we can take a look at them through her eyes:

The French system centred around the Divisional Ambulance in the field (the equivalent of the British flying hospital so lamentably missing since the Peninsular War). Their

The gale off the Port of Balaclava, 14 November, 1854,
mentioned by Sarah Anne in her journal

Commissariat difficulties at Kadikoi on the road from
Balaclava to Sebastopol during the wet weather

regimental medical service was little more than a first aid post which treated only those casualties exempted from duty for a day or two. The more seriously wounded and ill were evacuated to the Divisional Ambulance where those likely to recover in a matter of weeks were retained, while the rest were sent back to the general hospitals at base (in this case Constantinople). The French Sisters of Charity were not allowed in the Divisional Ambulances because, so it was rumoured, of the corruption of the French Intendance upon whom the Sisters quietly exercised a most unwelcome surveillance. (The Intendance was the civilian administration in charge of the medical services. Its corruption was legendary and during the Napoleonic wars it had been in constant conflict with the medical officers who were then, as in the Crimea, completely under its thumb.) The Sisters served in the French general hospitals in Constantinople where, apparently, they did all the cooking for the officers and that of the extras for the men. Florence Nightingale observed that they seemed more like 'consolatrices' in the wards, but with admirable housekeeping qualities. They did, however, have some nursing duties as is shown by their visiting her at Scutari to see how she coped with bed-sores (a curse in all the hospitals) and to borrow air pillows and water beds.

The Russian system of nursing seemed, to Florence Nightingale, by far the best she had known and to be the only perfectly organized system in the Crimean War. A Sister had charge of everything relating to the bedside care of the patient; she received her orders from the medical officer, attending him on his rounds and conferring with him afterwards. She was even responsible for the 'felchers', or dressers, and for the orderlies so far as their bedside conduct and duties were concerned. Away from the bedside, the felchers were under a senior felcher who in turn was under a medical officer; and in all that pertained to discipline, clothing, meals, and so forth, the orderlies were under the control of a non-commissioned officer.

The 'nurses' were of two sorts: there were the Sisters of the Elevation of the Cross who were generally widows of officers, though a few were Sisters of Charity. They had been formed by the Grand Duchess Helena Pavlovna and placed by her under the orders of the famous civilian surgeon Nikolai Ivanovich Pirogoff,[31] to whom had been given supreme surgical command in Sebastopol. Under these Sisters were the female nurses who were usually wives or widows of soldiers.

Completely distinct from the sisters and nurses were the 'Frauen des Barmherzigen Wittwen Instituts'. These Widows, roughly equivalent to the Ladies, had been instituted some forty years previously by Mary of Württemberg, for many years the venerated Empress-Mother. Florence Nightingale thought it possible that the pressures of war rendered their services rather nondescript as they were neither Sisters nor nurses, and perhaps, as she waggishly remarked, because they did not come under his orders, Professor Pirogoff had not a good word to say for them.

This, then, was the quality of the other two important medical services. Yet the Crimean War was a significantly greater medical disaster for their armies than it was for the British. The death rates per thousand from disease were: British, 119.3; French, 253.5 (the highest in history); Russians, 161.3.[32] The Russians, who had twice as many killed and wounded as the allies put together, suffered terribly from infected wounds and hospital gangrene raged through their wards. Pirogoff knew that segregating the patients would help stem the epidemic but he could not shift authority and so antagonized the government with his criticisms that he was compelled to resign his professorship at St. Petersburg. More than 14,000 Russians died of their wounds, compared with 1,800 British and 4,300 French.

However, the change that Florence Nightingale brought about is strikingly illuminated by comparing the figures for deaths from disease (excluding cholera) in 1854 and 1856. In 1854 there were 2,373 British who died and 1,857 French. In

1856 the figures were 17,129 French (an alarming number that was in part accounted for by a severe epidemic of typhus—a louse-borne disease that typically occurs in overcrowded, unhygenic conditions) and only 218 British.[33]

During her years of uncertainty, Florence Nightingale had acquired a detailed understanding of the principles of sanitation and it was the inspired way she succeeded in having these applied in the hospitals at Scutari (and later, in 1855, in the Crimea) that made the transformation possible. No amount of determination, or of political influence, or of public outrage on their own could have achieved these results. Nor indeed could the presence of female nurses, as evidenced by the misfortunes of the French and Russians. Florence Nightingale went to Scutari as an administrator; to achieve her purpose she had to have nurses who would obey her will. Sarah Anne and the others in that original small party were the essential instruments of her genius.

MEDICAL SUPPLIES

The problems besetting Dr. Andrew Smith, Director General of the Army Medical Department were many. The Department had been eroded by forty years of Treasury miserliness, and economy had become both a way of life and a state of mind. Smith, in his office in London, had a staff of two medical officers and four clerks and in consequence had to deal with a whole mass of petty detail that should never have reached his desk. The red tape that bound him was unbelievably tangled. For instance, the only direct financial control he had was in the purchase of medicines, dressings, and surgical appliances. On matters of policy he had to approach the Military Secretary to the Commander-in-Chief at the Horse Guards and the Secretary *for* War (responsible for overall civilian supervision of the army); for approval of expenditure on equipment and supplies he had to go to the Secretary *at* War (Sidney Herbert —he was responsible for army finance and administration). But the procedure for obtaining medical comforts[34] took the prize:

'If the Director General of the Army Medical Department wished to furnish our hospitals in the East some kinds of supplies, as for instance, wine, sago, arrowroot, he had to send his purpose revolving in an orrery of official bodies: For first, he well knew, he must move the Horse Guards, and the Horse Guards must move the Ordnance, and the Ordnance must set going the Admiralty, and the Admiralty must give orders to the Victualling Office, and the Victualling Office must concert measures with the Transport Office, and the Transport Office (having only three transports) must appeal to the private ship-owners, in the hope that sooner or later they would furnish the sea-carriage needed.'[35]

Smith's position was at first well nigh intolerable. The Crimea, thanks to the telegraph, was on his doorstep so far as trouble was concerned, but when it came to an accurate understanding of events and an assessment of the appropriate action to take it was still as remote as Timbuctoo. The new dimension that had been added to warfare could only be mastered by experience. And, to make matters worse, Smith was often kept in the dark about important military decisions.

The Russians had been at war with the Turks since October 1853 and had occupied Turkish territory along the banks of the Danube. Britain did not declare war until March 27, 1854, after six weeks of hurried and inadequate preparation. Smith, however, had been warned on February 22 that troops already gathering in Malta might be sent east to help the Turks. He reacted by despatching three senior medical officers to the Balkans to report on the climate and prevalent diseases; their impressions, which came back during April, were decidedly unfavourable. The climate went to extremes during summer and winter; diseases such as malaria, dysentery, typhoid, and typhus, were endemic; and sanitation was non-existent. The reports also contained valuable recommendations for preserving the health of the troops which Smith passed on to the Military Secretary only to see them rejected.

Setting the Scene

From the moment of the warning Smith began fighting his way through the administrative jungle in an attempt to ensure that the Department should not be found wanting. Bed coverage (the number of hospital beds likely to be required, expressed as a percentage of the total force) was reckoned to be adequate at about 10 per cent except at times of fighting or epidemic disease when 20–25 per cent was thought to be more realistic. The provision of these beds was traditionally the responsibility of the principal medical officer on the spot—in this case, Dr. John Hall—but Smith thought he would play safe and sent in a requisition for 5,000 beds. However, as the requisition had to be initiated by a non-existent purveyors department, a retired purveyor was added to Smith's staff. The requisition then had to get the approval of the Commander-in-Chief before it could be met by the Board of Ordnance. About half the beds had arrived by June, but the full number did not reach Turkey until Christmas Eve—a delay due to poor delivery by the contractors and severe pressure on shipping space.

Next, Smith set in motion the request for hospital equipment only to find there was none in store (no one had foreseen the need for a general hospital) and again it all had to be ordered from civilian contractors. In fact the only supplies ready for shipment in time were the medicines, dressings, and surgical equipment ordered by Smith himself from the Apothecaries Hall—and due to the shortage of ships, they sat on the quayside from February 17 till April 3. As all medical stores were loaded under the orders of the Ordnance Officer at the Tower of London into shipping allocated by the Naval Transport Officer, it is scarcely surprising that priority was given to military materials. Nevertheless, a ship did sail on April 11 containing the complete equipment for a hospital of 550 beds as well as spare blankets and sheets together with marquees and bedding for the regimental hospitals. Admittedly it was well below the coverage needed for an army of 25–28,000 men but it was the best that could be done.

Smith was also busy seeing to the regimental needs for the treatment and evacuation of casualties in the field. He ordered 40 ambulance carts, both two- and four-wheeled (relying, as had been the practice in the Peninsular War, on local requisitioning for any further carts that might be needed), four large waggons containing stores, 300 stretchers, regimental panniers, cases of instruments, bandages, splints, everything in fact that was required. But when, early in April, the army arrived in Turkey, its medical supplies had still not left England. The regimental surgeons at Scutari were fortunate in being able to take over the Turkish supplies and equipment in the General Hospital, but those in Gallipoli had nothing. And nothing that Smith had ordered for them reached the regiments until June. However, during May three ships did arrive in Turkey with hospital stores and equipment.

Yet, back in London, Smith believed that all was well and that the army now had medical materials sufficient to last for six months; he relied on Hall to keep him informed of developments locally and to indent for further supplies as necessary.

Unfortunately, even when stores eventually left England some items such as blankets, brandy, and port, were liable to go missing, and comforts generally were used up in less than three months largely owing to short ordering by Smith's purveyor. Moreover, as the labelling was left to the Ordnance Officer the stores were frequently addressed to inappropriate personnel who made little or no attempt to dispose of them correctly. When this fact dawned on Smith he addressed everything to senior medical officers personally, but by the time the consignment arrived the nominee had quite likely moved elsewhere. To combat the transport delays Smith should have marked the requisitions for stores 'Urgent' because as Captain A. Milne, R.N., of the Admiralty said in his evidence to the Roebuck Committee, had he seen anything so marked he would have sent them out as hastily as possible by steamer.[36]

Milne's evidence also exposed a shameful blunder over hospital ships. On May 11, Smith had asked the Military Secretary for a liberal supply of well ventilated ships with ample accommodation to be used as floating hospitals, and for the evacuation of casualties to Scutari and the transport of invalids home to England.[37] Yet Milne declared that the Admiralty had never received such a requisition; though when asked whether he considered it a part of his duty to suggest such a thing, he replied, 'No. I thought of it, I must acknowledge, and I must acknowledge that I thought it odd that a requisition was not made.'[38] Somewhere along the line, someone had evidently lost or ignored the request. The consequences for the sick and wounded were beyond description and the waste of medicines and supplies arising from the need to equip available transports as temporary hospital ships was deplorable.

At the end of May the army, under Lord Raglan, set out for the Black Sea port of Varna in Bulgaria. The troops were in good heart and eager to drive the Russians out of the occupied territories. As it happened, they never saw the Russians who left of their own accord; instead they met all the diseases forecast by Smith's medical officers and took not the slightest precautions against them—despite the fact that the principles of sound sanitary conduct for an army in the field were well known and had been so for a hundred years.[39]

Varna was a sordid insanitary place and the dilapidated building chosen as the general hospital was in keeping with its surroundings. The hospital equipment, sent on from Scutari, arrived on June 3 but the bed cover was only 10 per cent which was marginal even if conditions proved favourable. The army moved inland and camped overlooking marshy ground (thus inviting malaria). Its medical equipment had arrived by this time, though most units chose to leave their large medicine chests behind in Varna. Inevitably, fevers and bowel diseases soon became epidemic and, most disastrous of all, cholera appeared. The regimental surgeons quickly ran out of medicines, and because of shortage of transport the authorities refused to send them their medicine chests. The hospital at Varna was overwhelmed.

By the end of July, despite serious doubts about the health of the army, it was decided to invade the Crimea. Hall was not told about this officially but on the strength of rumour he asked the quartermaster-general for conveyance for 400 tons of stores plus the waggons, men, and horses of the ambulance train; the vessels should then be kept as hospital ships. Hall had to fight every inch of the way, first to get transport from the Commissariat to carry stores to the quay, then to persuade the Agent of Transport to provide boats to carry them out to the waiting *John Masterman* which already was loaded with the complete equipment for a 600-bed hospital as well as reserves of medicines, dressings, and a small amount of medical comforts. However, only three of the ambulances were taken on board and nowhere in the remainder of the fleet could Hall find space for the others. He protested strongly but to no avail. Also sailing from Varna were *Cambria* and *Andes*, both equipped as hospital ships yet both too small to be really effective for the evacuation of casualties. Two thousand men were left at Varna either sick or dead.

When Hall sailed on September 4, stores were still arriving from England—no one had told Smith that Varna was being abandoned. To make matters worse, the stocks at Scutari had fallen dangerously low as Ward, the purveyor, was keeping no records and had not asked Hall for replenishments. Nevertheless Hall himself took no steps to re-route unwanted supplies from Varna until just before he left when he ordered a recent shipment to be loaded on *Bombay* and sent to Scutari. He also wrote a brusque note to Ward telling him to indent on Varna for whatever equipment he might need. But even this apparently excellent idea fell foul of the system, as perhaps Hall should have realized it would.

Ward did as he was told and on September 6 and again ten days later wrote to the purveyor at Varna urging him to despatch without delay as many beds and as much equipment as he could spare. The letters lay undelivered in the office of Rear-Admiral Boxer, Principal Naval Officer at Constantinople, because he did not consider the request to be urgent. In November he did, however, send a ship to Varna and the equipment eventually reached Scutari at the end of the month. Admiral Boxer was also responsible for creating a shortage of medicines and dressings at Scutari by sending a shipment, that arrived in Turkey in September, on to Varna simply because it was labelled Varna and regardless of the fact that he knew the army had already left.

When the British army invaded the Crimea in the middle of September it had no transport so, true to Peninsular tradition, 350 local carts were rounded up, 24 of which were given to Hall. He kept six and distributed the other 18 throughout the army to carry the reserves of medicines brought by *John Masterman*. But there were no proper ambulances, not even the three sent from Varna: one had disappeared and the other two were without their horses. Then, unbelievably, Lord Raglan ordered that no regimental hospital equipment was to be carried in the advance on Sebastopol; the regimental surgeons were limited to a pair of panniers, a small box of medical comforts, and a bell tent. In other words, while facilities for first-aid were carried, there was not a single hospital bed for the entire army. And the men were ordered to leave their knapsacks behind at Kalamita Bay where they landed.

Disease continued to ravage the army and the sick had to be evacuated. Such transport ships as happened to be available were pressed into service, much to the disgust of their captains; they were invariably grossly overcrowded and inadequately staffed and equipped. Moreover, since a transport was rarely used for sick or wounded more than once the equipment and medical supplies that were carried were dumped at the end of the voyage. Particularly distressing for men suffering from cholera and dysentery was the shortage of bedpans and urinals. It is difficult to know whose hell was the worse: that of the men cramped between decks or of those who spent the four or five day journey lying unattended on the open deck. In one shipload of 430 sick men (mostly suffering from cholera) 114 died during the voyage.

After the battle of the Alma on September 20, the British had 1,800 wounded, some of whom were not brought in for 48 hours. The surgical operations were carried out under horrifyingly primitive conditions with doors torn from their hinges to serve instead of the operating tables left behind at Kalamita Bay. The one saving grace was chloroform which, contrary to some stories, was used quite freely. Hall was then faced with the problem of getting the casualties to the beaches as he had no ambulances and no medical officers for escort duty. Fortunately the Navy and the French came to the rescue with transport, but Hall had to take some of the regimental surgeons to staff the transport ships though he could do nothing about the lack of orderlies on board. This problem of transport to Scutari persisted into December. On the 17th of that month Hall was eventually allocated two fully equipped steamers that ran a regular service between Balaclava and Scutari, but as they only held 150 men each he acquired on December 24 another four ships, all well equipped, supplied, and staffed.

When, at the beginning of October, the allies were encamped around Sebastopol, the British sent to Kalamita Bay for their regimental hospitals and stores only to find that the bulk had been spirited away. Mercifully, Hall was able to establish a hospital at Balaclava to cope with the sick and to hold the casualties awaiting transport to Scutari. This hospital consisted of the local school and two marquees; it had on average 300–350 patients and was kept fully equipped and supplied from the stores on board *John Masterman*.

For the battles of Balaclava (October 25) and Inkerman (November 5) Hall had obtained 12 ambulance waggons; his only regret was that he had not managed to acquire the full 40 originally sent out. Unhappily, though, these two battles made Hall feel that his hospital was no longer safe for long-term casualties and he evacuated 2,000 men to Scutari. He knew this would strain the Scutari resources but he naively assumed that Menzies would by then have received the stores from Varna.

On November 14 a fresh disaster struck. Previously the weather in the Crimea had been mild with mist and rain, but in the early hours of the fourteenth the violent storm recorded by Sarah Anne struck the Crimea. The loss of *Prince* with all hands was catastrophic for the army as she carried the winter underwear and other warm clothing for the entire force—it almost seems as though some evil genius was at work, since the clothing should have been despatched much earlier except that no one in London could make up their minds whether the army would have to winter in the Crimea or not. Lord Raglan admittedly sent at once to the quartermaster-general's department in Constantinople for whatever warm clothing they could buy, but despite two shipments that arrived from England during December, the last man did not get his full winter issue until January. And yet greatcoats and skin rugs were stored in some of the other ships that survived the storm—they were not issued because no one knew they were there.

Clothing was not the only valuable cargo to go down in *Prince*. She was also carrying desperately needed medicines (including 300 pounds of opium) for Scutari, but they had not been unloaded there because they had been packed underneath ammunition destined for Balaclava.

The storm also played havoc with communications (not to mention living conditions) ashore. The dirt road from Balaclava became a mud bath and the resulting difficulties of transport persisted throughout the winter. Virtually everything had to be carried the three or so miles by men up to their thighs in mud. Men could ill be spared from military duties either to restore communications or to carry supplies; in consequence the troops grew weaker and fell sick, thus further reducing their effectiveness. Even when help was provided something inevitably seemed to go wrong; for instance, a large cargo of vegetables arrived in November but the men found it difficult to carry and so most just rotted in the hold. Again, on November 17 Smith ordered 40,000 gallons of lime juice to be distributed throughout the winter to prevent scurvy; 20,000 gallons arrived in early December but due to an administrative error it was not distributed for another two months.

To conclude this sorry tale of disasters, the pieces of which were picked up at Scutari, we discover that suits of hospital clothing, boards and trestles for beds, and other miscellaneous items such as knives, forks, plates, and cups were in store at Balaclava but the regimental surgeons were unaware of their existence—nothing was issued, everything had to be indented for. Hall reckoned, however, that by mid-January the troops in the field had all that they required. But the damage had been done; sickness continued to tear the army apart and only the arrival of better weather and the Sanitary Commission was able to bring this under control.

Hall's failure from the start had been in not keeping his superior in London fully informed. Whether from inability or unwillingness he failed to send back accurate appreciations of the changing situation. As a result Smith knew nothing of the transport and shipping difficulties and of their aggravation by the large numbers of sick; he learnt of shortages only through other sources and did not know what to make of them as Hall was silent on the subject. In desperation he decided to communicate directly with Menzies.

Menzies meantime had been coping adequately with his job of medical superintendent at Scutari despite his problems with the purveyor. When *Bombay* arrived from Varna in September loaded with 5,200 sheets, 3,500 blankets, 1,700 rugs and palliasses, and more than 1,000 sets of hospital clothing, he was almost equipped to deal with the 2,000 patients for whom he had accommodation—the missing items were a thousand or so of the beds ordered by Smith that had been sent to Varna. His medical staff consisted of himself (he was responsible for all the major operations), one staff surgeon, 17 staff assistant surgeons, and three local civilian doctors. They were already at full stretch dealing with the sick when the casualties from the Alma arrived; only by commandeering the services of 17 regimental surgeons and 10 naval surgeons from the transports was he able to meet the challenge. At this stage, too, he was just able to avoid serious overcrowding by the use of the convalescent hulks in the harbour. These ships served a valuable purpose as they freed beds in the hospitals for new arrivals. Unfortunately though, transports frequently arrived without warning and before space could be cleared for the casualties by the transfer of convalescents to the hulks. The casualties were nevertheless disembarked—a move that simply reinforced the picture of misery and chaos.

On October 18, at the height of the furore created by Russell's despatches, Smith wrote to Menzies telling him that if the reported shortages of lint, linen, and medicines were correct, he should purchase them at once with funds made available to the British Ambassador in Constantinople. The Ambassador, Lord Stratford de Redcliffe, on the instruction of the Foreign Office, offered Menzies directly any financial assistance he might need. Menzies refused, saying the hospitals were perfectly well supplied and that, in any case, he was daily expecting additional stores from England and Varna. The next ship from England did not arrive until November 28, the same time as the Varna stores eventually reached Scutari. Menzies' refusal seems inexplicable though he may have been wary of this strange channel of communication and have seen himself having to pay the bill in the end. So, instead of accepting the offer he made a desperate plea to Admiral Boxer on November 5 to send to Varna for stores which, as we have seen, was successful. However, when the ship returned on November 21, for some reason she was not unloaded until the first week in December. By early November, too, Smith realized that his beds had either not yet left England or were on tour around the area and so he ordered another 2,000 followed by 4,000 more a month later—sufficient to bring the bed coverage up to 30 per cent—but they only arrived between

February and May 1855 at a slower rate than the influx of casualties.

Thankfully the whole system started to become more human towards the end of 1854, largely due to the efforts of Sidney Herbert. The purveyor at Scutari (a Mr. Wreford who had replaced Ward during October) was subordinated to the orders of the medical staff in everything concerned with the welfare of the sick, which meant that he could no longer be obstructive on financial grounds. Medicines could also be issued without the counter-signature of the medical superintendent. In December Smith's need to 'send his purpose revolving in an orrery of official bodies' was brought to an end by order of the Secretary for War and he was thus able to buy medical comforts direct from the contractor. He was soon after permitted to obtain his other medical supplies through the Commissariat Department which had been removed from Treasury control and placed under the War Office. Then on December 29 the Duke of Newcastle (the Secretary for War) ordered that 200 tons of medical comforts and medicines should be sent, with priority, every fortnight until the middle of March; thus, after the end of January, Florence Nightingale's own stores were no longer needed. And finally the transport difficulties and delays were overcome by the creation of a Transport Board which took over the roles played by the Admiralty and the Ordnance Board.

In February 1855 the Hospital Commissioners submitted their report. Their recommendations for improving the administration at Scutari were put into effect without delay and as the war dragged on most of their other advice was acted upon. Then, on March 6, the Sanitary Commission descended upon the hospitals at Scutari; it had powers to act and under its guidance these hospitals—and later the others in the area— were brought up to thoroughly acceptable hygienic standards.

But by the time all this had been achieved, Sarah Anne was home in England. She had known only the horror of Scutari, a horror that in her own way and as a member of Florence

Nightingale's 'own old party' she had done her best to alleviate. Innocent of all the background politicking, she tells the story of that winter of 1854–5 in terms that everyone can understand, the human terms, the terms that matter.

Embarkation of the sick at Balaclava

The General Hospital, Scutari

The Barrack Hospital, Scutari

SARAH ANNE'S JOURNAL

On Friday, 20th October 1854, while walking by Stoke Damerel Church with our orphans, about 3 P.M., we met Anna, who put in my hands a note from Sister Emma, bidding me go at once to Plymouth. I gave the children into her care and went.

On reaching Windham Place, Sister Emma told me she had received a telegram to send me, Sister Bertha, and Sister Amelia to London. So we left Plymouth by the 5 P.M. mail train. At Totnes, Margaret[1] joined us, having received a similar message at Asherne, and posted thence just in time to catch our train. At Bristol, Clara joined. We made conjectures as to our destiny, but wide from the truth. Having heard of an outbreak of cholera in London, we fancied we were going to nurse there.

We reached London about 4 A.M., and drove to Osnaburg Street.[2] There, Sisters Catherine, Elizabeth,[3] and Clara received us affectionately, but did not enlighten us as to our destination. In about an hour I was sent to the Superior, who looked ill and exhausted, scarcely able to speak. She said shortly, and with effort, 'Our soldiers in the East want nurses —some are going—I wish to send eight—are you willing to be one?'

Sarah Anne's Journal

Gladly I answered 'Yes,' and went away.

As I rejoined the sisters, Sister Bertha said she knew it was some pleasant mission, I looked so happy. I did feel thankful and happy, both for such interesting work, and to escape trial and perplexity I had been enduring.

21st October.—At 7 A.M. we went to bed, and to sleep, though told that in two hours we must rise and go to Sidney Herbert (Secretary at War) for his directions. Accordingly within two hours we rose and drove to Belgrave Square. There, after waiting a time, we received our papers of agreement, and with the other nurses received instructions from Mr Sidney Herbert. He spoke of our duties—of modesty and propriety, of enduring hardness, and of carefully avoiding religious proselytising; and ended by thanking us for being willing to engage in an office which must be trying, but which might be a very great comfort to the poor men who had suffered for their country, and so deserved consideration. He spoke well.

There we met Miss Nightingale, and from the first moment I felt an impulse to love, trust, and respect her. Her appearance and manner impressed me with a sense of goodness and wisdom, of high mental powers highly cultivated and devoted to highest ends.

On leaving Mr Herbert's we returned to Osnaburg Street. A lady at Mr Herbert's gave us each a railroad rug, which did good service. We spent the rest of the day in preparatory needlework.

22nd October.—Sunday, we received Holy Communion at St Mary Magdalene (Munster Square), and in the evening we were put under the charge of Miss Langston, head of St Saviour's, London, Sisterhood.

23rd October.—About 6 A.M., we left St Saviour's for London Bridge Station, where we met again our sister nurses, about thirty in number, and five nuns, not in any conventual costume, but in simple black dresses. Mrs and Mr Bracebridge were there, and went with us. Miss Nightingale had preceded us to Paris.

We had a hurried breakfast at Folkstone (*sic*), and then went on board the Boulogne packet. As the boat left the pier, the crowd, knowing our destination, gave us three hearty cheers, and quickly the coast of England receded from sight. Some expressed sentiments of regretful affection, but soon all such emotions were put to flight, and sounds and sights of physical distress succeeded. Miss Langston and I alone established our character as good sailors; the rest of our party, with the nuns and nurses, all proved themselves unable to withstand the disastrous effects of a swell in the English Channel. But these sufferings were soon over, and we stood rather giddy on the pier at Boulogne. We walked to the hotel, where a very tasteful display of French cookery awaited us, for which the host refused payment. The poor merry-hearted porter-women also insisted on carrying our luggage without payment.

After resting a few hours, we proceeded to Paris, which we reached late at night. I was too tired and confused, from a succession of disturbed nights, to remember much of our circumstances, but I remember we each gladly retired to a neat clean little white-curtained French bed.

24th October.—We rose early, and after breakfast met an addition to our party—the five nuns from Bermondsey, who (as soon as they knew that their services would not be rejected by Government) had been sent off by their ecclesiastical superiors, but had waited for us at Paris, being required to do so by telegram from Mr Sidney Herbert, which reached them there. I was much struck by the appearance of one of these nuns—her pale face, expressive countenance, and dark grey eyes were very interesting. She seemed to me in appearance the very beau ideal of a nun as she first appeared in the grey early dawn, and further acquaintance only deepened the interest she excited, though not in all points fulfilling the idea her saintly sort of beauty expressed. Her convent name was Sister Mary de Gonzaga.[4] The manners of these five nuns were very pleasing, there was no gloom, no formality, no self-consciousness apparent; animated, simple, affectionate, and humble, they seemed to be indeed living epistles of the Gospel of Jesus Christ known and read of all with whom they had intercourse. Surely their superiors had wisely chosen in selecting them for this mission, for certainly their conduct did much to disarm dislike, and to gain proselytes to their cause. It was sad to us to find that at least two of them, and they the most striking and attractive of the five, had been children of the Church of England.

We drove through Paris a little before seven, and took the railway to Lyons. We dined at one of the stations. On starting after dinner, one of the officials, a policeman or porter, having heard who we were, addressed Miss Langston:

'Ah, madame, que je voudrais être un de vos malades afin que vous me rappeleriez à la vie' and was very anxious not to waste his politeness, asking each of us, 'Entendez vous ce que je dis.' On assuring him we did, he begged leave in English to shake hands, and said 'Good-bye.'

We reached Lyons in the evening, and passed the night in an hotel.

25th October.—Early in the morning we went down the Rhone to Valence by boat. The country seemed beautiful, though the weather was wet and misty.

26th October.—From Valence we proceeded by train to Marseilles.

27th October.—As we had nothing to do, and could not go out, these days were somewhat dreary, and our meals, being the chief event of the day and breaking its monotony, acquired undue importance. The rest of the day was spent in needle-work in our larger bedroom, and in silence. So the signal for meals was very welcome when we went along intricate passages, down stairs, and through a garden which led to the *salle à manger*, where we found assembled the nuns and nurses, Mrs Bracebridge presiding.

In the morning five persons appeared in a conventual dress of coarse white serge, with the linen head-dress of nuns. They looked very conspicuous, and to me far from attractive; their dress seemed coarse and ill-shaped, and gave them altogether a ghastly and ungainly appearance. I did not feel inclined to rejoice in this acquisition to our party, and wondered whence they had sprung. On examining them more minutely I thought I knew some of their faces, and on looking round at the rest of our party found the five Norwood nuns in simple black dress had disappeared, these white figures taking their place. Considering these facts, and recalling the features of our departed companions, the result was a conviction that the quiet well-behaved ladies in black who had accompanied us from London still existed, and seemed to purpose continuing with us in a new and to my mind by no means an improved form. Some of us could hardly be persuaded they were the same.

We sailed from Marseilles in the *Vectis*. It was a bright sunny evening, but the superstitious among us attributed the distress and mishaps of our voyage to our beginning each stage of our journey on a Friday. Going to the *Vectis* in small boats, when we got on deck we found ourselves in a little steamer, and were at once introduced to our quarters, which were in the fore-cabin, where there were berths for forty, which we fully occupied. They were divided into little recesses, each containing four berths like little shelves. We [the Sellonites] had the two innermost recesses nearest the forepart of the boat, of course the most confined and farthest from fresh air, though the most retired. The nuns had a little division for themselves at the foot of the cabin stairs. The nurses lay between. In bad weather the nuns were best off for air, though they paid for this advantage by having a double allowance of water which the boat constantly shipped, and which washed over the deck and came down the cabin stairs.[5] Till overcome by sickness, Sister Mary de Gonzaga was kept pretty busy swabbing up. Miss Nightingale being a very bad sailor, retired as soon as we got on board. Among our fellow-passengers were several doctors.

Sister Bertha, knowing her tendency to sea-sickness, disappeared as soon as we got on board, and took possession of her berth, where she remained the whole voyage in much suffering, yet most calm and cheerful, taking a composed and bright view of our forlorn and rather desperate circumstances. Miss Langston, Sister Elizabeth, and I were in the same compartment with her, the four others of our party in the one opposite. My shelf was above Sister Bertha's, but I passed only one night in it, preferring from experience of its horrors to dispense with bed altogether rather than to lie down in a close little box like a coffin, narrow and devoid of air, but full of crawling creatures. During the intervals of her sickness Sister Bertha employed herself in a general massacre, so that before we finished our voyage she had nearly exterminated the inhabitants of her division; but the remedy seemed worse than the disease—dead and dying bugs worse and more offensive than those in the full vigour of life and in active exercise of their energies and faculties. So I left mine in undisturbed possession, and spent my nights on the cabin floor.

Soon after we left Marseilles the sun set, but most of us remained on deck till it was dark, dreading the closeness of the cabin. But the weather being calm, we were able to keep the skylight open, and passed a comparatively tolerable night. Two boys acted as *filles de chambre* to the victims in the *Vectis*' second cabin whose state became gradually increasingly distressing. Several were from the first confined there by sickness.

28th October.—In the morning we passed through the Straits of Bonifacio. The coast on either side seemed rocky, barren, and precipitous. On leaving the Straits a little sea rose. The *Vectis* was a swift sailor, but not fitted for a rough open sea. Saturday was a fine day, though rather breezy. Towards evening, as the sick were lying exhausted in their berths, having eaten nothing, they heard a refreshing clatter announcing tea at the other end of the cabin, and began to indulge in visions of the relief a cup of tea would afford, and to form hopes of its reaching them. These hopes being delayed, they raised a feeble cry for 'tea,' but in vain—it was not heard—no one thought of them; no tea reached them—and they had to exercise patience and resignation.

We who were not sick kept as much as we could out of the cabin for fear of joining their number, and so were absent when this trial occurred. Sister Bertha bore it bravely. Sister Ethelreda, who suffered exceedingly from exhaustion and want of air, had recourse to Eau de Cologne, and told me she preserved her life by drinking it. The lads who were our attendants were not negligent, but with forty women to wait on, mostly sick, they could not do much. The sick were in general patient and unexacting. Mrs Hodges, one of St John's nurses,[6] was very unwearied in waiting on her sick companions. Those of our party who were well—Miss Langston, Miss Erskine, and I—sat on deck all night in preference to enduring our close cabin, and aggravating the sufferings of the sick. Miss Nightingale and a lady who landed at Malta also lay on mattresses on deck all night.

29th October.—Sunday was fine. It did not seem like Sunday: no service, and the sailors seemed more than usually busy preparing to land cargo at Malta. We again remained on deck that night.

30th October.—Before daybreak we reached Malta. Soon the boat was surrounded by noisy Maltese boatmen offering their services, and a little after daybreak Mr B. [Bracebridge] appeared and invited us to go on shore. Five nuns, seven of us, and almost all the nurses went. Our boat followed Mr B.'s, which seemed running out to sea, but it turned a point and ran into a bay, where we landed on the rocks with a little difficulty; one nurse plumped into the water, but scrambled out without injury beyond a wetting. On shore we were immediately surrounded by noisy guides offering their services. Mr B. seemed to understand them perfectly, and with equally noisy rebuffs got rid of them, and took the office on himself, marshalling us in procession—black sisters in front, white sisters in rear, nurses intermediate. So we marched through the town, Mr B. running on before and chatting to every respectable person he met, and announcing to them our meaning—'Nuns, ladies, and nurses going to nurse the soldiers of the British army in the Crimea.'

The Church of St John's Knights, to which he took us, was very beautiful and gorgeous, but I was too tired to admire it much, and felt annoyed at being guilty of gaping irreverence in walking about and gazing while Mass was being celebrated, though the kneeling congregation seemed quite undisturbed. The nuns naturally joined the worshippers, though Mr B. remonstrated, and threatened to leave them behind. At last they left the unfinished service, and returned with us in the same order as before, under Mr B.'s command, who seemed quite at home in the Mediterranean,[7] and kindly anxious that we should see and be seen as much as possible.

'Halt!'

'To the right face!'

'Advance!'

'Halt!'

'Halt!' he shouted, while we meekly obeyed to the best of our bewildered understandings. We were weary with sleepless nights, and though so early, the sun was dazzling and oppressive, and there seemed a white blaze from bare rocks, and a great want of shade; so we were glad to get back to the little *Vectis*, which soon left Malta and advanced to our destination.

We spent the day on deck, occasionally going down to the cabin, where the sick again began to accumulate, and when unwelcome night came on we were preparing to spend it on deck, when a message came from Miss N. requesting us not to do so, and a gale rising rendered it impossible; so a little after dark I retired to our cabin, falling down on the way from the ship's motion. Sister Elizabeth had gone a little before, and seeming unsafe in her movements, the little French courier politely offered his arm for her support, but in vain, for as they crossed the deck a sudden lurch laid them both flat on the deck.

'It comes worser and worser, I tink,' said the poor courier, scrambling up on his feet.

When I reached the cabin I found the skylight closed and covered with sailcloth. It was never again opened, and as it was the only legitimate entrance for light or air, both were carefully excluded; consequently the air was very foul, the floor wet (for no efforts could entirely exclude the water), and thickly strewed with sick women. Three of our party, Sisters Elizabeth, Harriet Erskine, and Margaret, lay there, and I joined them. One of the officers came down to bid us keep up our hearts and not be alarmed, for the gale was rising, and we should have a noisy night. Most of the nurses promised to behave well, and notwithstanding the noise, most soon seemed in a quiet sleep. I had no inclination for sleep, though wearied, wet, and cold. I sat listening to the whistling wind, praying the Lord Almighty to grant us a quiet night and a Christian end.

30th October.—A little after midnight the noise increased, and one wakeful timid nurse rose and went to the bottom of the cabin stairs. Seeing her nervous trepidation, I begged her to sit down quietly by me, but she would not, and soon after a fearful noise began on deck, as if the men were dragging chains. The poor nurse thought this preliminary to the sailors escaping and leaving us to be lost, and she uttered a fearful shriek, and then a burst of wild cries for 'Mercy this once, only this once.' The nurses being roused from sleep, took up the cry, and 'Mercy, mercy, Lord, have mercy,' resounded on all sides as they hurriedly arose and began to dress.

In vain I tried to quiet them, and then went to the head of our party and begged her to use her efforts to soothe and quiet them, but she said very composedly:

'I have no authority: I cannot interfere.'

I feared their going on deck and being washed overboard, or puzzling and disturbing the sailors at their work. Meanwhile Mrs C.[8] addressed them in a tranquillising tone:

'We are not flying from the face of the Almighty, nor from His work; if we die it is in a good cause, and God won't let us perish in vain.'

One nurse, who seemed calm, and boasted to be an old

sailor, volunteered to go up and find out 'all about it.' She soon returned and quieted the others by assuring them the sailors had not left the ship, nor intended doing so, that we had run upon several rocks, but the *Vectis* being a good ship, no harm was done as yet. I do not know how she obtained this information, which seemed to satisfy the nurses, though my only satisfaction was in knowing that she was talking nonsense. However, the panic subsided, though many spent the remainder of the night in prayer and some on their knees. One prayed aloud in Welsh, and expressed her regret that we could not benefit by the beautiful words she was uttering.

By return of daylight our spirits rose, and Sister Elizabeth and I attempted to leave our dismal cabin, which was becoming a chamber of horrors. Though still rough, the storm was less violent. The poor sailors seemed tired and wet, but cheerful and good tempered. As we two, tired, dirty, and rather miserable, stood at the top of the cabin stairs, Sister Elizabeth asked one of the sailors to fill us a cup with the water which was freely washing over the deck. We could not wash below; it was difficult to stand, and we could not reach the basins without incommoding the sick. He good humouredly filled our cup, and dipping the corner of a handkerchief in the salt water and rubbing it over our face and hands, we did all our circumstances permitted in the way of toilet, and then took the opportunity of a lull to cross the deck and stagger over to the stern, where we passed the day.

I felt too worn out and the passage across the deck too dangerous to attempt it often, and so left the sick a good deal to themselves, especially as I could not supply their chief want, that of fresh air. However, I went once, and found as usual Sister Bertha very sick but cheerful and uncomplaining, Sister Ethelreda suffering from exhaustion and want of air; both in their dark narrow recess. Clara lay on the wet floor, whither she had moved in order to give Sister Ethelreda more breathing space, and there she lay on the floor, soaking up to the neck (in sea water happily), day after day, without food and almost without air, till really speechless and half dead. The sea was still washing the deck and gently pouring into our cabin, though every effort was made to exclude it. It was a dismal scene, the dark wet cabin, with one miserable swinging light, just enough to show the sick lying about in every direction.

In their own cabin at the bottom of the stairs lay the pale picturesque Sister Mary de Gonzaga; her eyes shut, lying straight on her back, she seemed a beautiful picture of death. However, it took a good deal, I should think, to overcome her. A few hours after she was up again, serving any who needed it, and keeping up the spirits of all by her cheerful playful manner. The others were not equally fearless, but all by their kind gentle manner, their endurance, and unselfish uncomplaining conduct were examples valuable to us all.

Night drew on again, and as it was calmer, I climbed into my shelf, and tried to sleep as I hardly had done since we sailed, and I felt weary and exhausted; but finding it impossible to rest there, I descended and lay on the floor.

31st *October*.—During the night the gale had risen again, and by morning it was higher than I had as yet seen it. We crossed the deck with difficulty, and sat at the stern end near the helmsman. We were passing some of the Greek islands, which looked barren and uninviting. Rough as it was, some of the sailors told us it would soon be worse, and so we found, for coming out of the shelter of an island the full force of the sea came against our little boat. We were going in the teeth of the wind, and instead of dancing over the great waves, our little quick sharp steamer cut right through them, and they washed over and seemed as if they would swallow her up. I looked for each approaching wave as for the last, and held fast. Weary and exhausted from want of food and rest, wet and cold (though not sea-sick), I thought if we are to be drowned, it will not be a long struggle for some of us.

We were invited to breakfast. Some bold hungry passengers went down, but I was too anxious and fearful to do so, so I declined. Pretty rosy Sister Jean de Chantel, who sat near me, honestly said, 'I am far too frightened to eat'; but I was too afraid to utter my fears. Soon after the ship's surgeon ordered a pailful of warm negus[9] to be made and carried round, and a tumblerful given to each. Certainly the effect was wonderful on our cold, wearied, wet, exhausted frames and depressed spirits. Hope revived, and life seemed worth living, and the waves did not seem so appalling, but we were still tired and dirty.

The sea splashing on our dresses and faces produced a curious effect. Drying in the folds and hollows of each, it left a crust of crystallised salt. Round Sister Elizabeth's eyes especially there was a thick white covering, and her bright dark eyes sparkling out of the snow-white caves looked striking and singular. She had more life and spirit than I had, and turning to me said, laughing:

'If we are to stay here much longer, I must certainly ask to be lashed to the ship, for I am tired of holding fast.'

Miss Nightingale was still ill in bed.

We went down to dinner, and remained below with Mrs Bracebridge, who interested us much with accounts of her past travels, voyages, and perils by land and water in Syria, Greece, and the Mediterranean. Her conversation, anecdotes, description of events and characters, were very interesting. They were no common powers of conversation which could so absorb us at a time of physical exhaustion and of mental anxiety. Though I had little further intercourse with Mrs Bracebridge, that evening convinced us that she was a strong, high-minded, large-hearted woman. She kept us deeply interested till late, when we retired to our cabin. H. Erskine remained, as Mrs B. offered her a berth in her cabin. H. E., like me, had not suffered from sea-sickness, but from exhaustion, want of sleep and of air. On reaching our cabin we found Sisters Bertha, Ethelreda, and Clara much as we had left them. Sisters Elizabeth, Margaret, and I lay down in our clothes near poor Clara.

1*st November.*—The storm increased, and though all the

others were so worn out and sunk in sleep as to disregard it, I lay awake listening and waiting for each shock, and expecting some crisis, for the motion of the ship seemed to me too violent to continue. And at last it came about midnight—a fearful crash, and then a pause. I started up, my heart quailed with the conviction we had at last struck, and were going down. It was an awful pause; the shock roused all, though being less wakeful, they rose more slowly, and as they rose a volume of water splashed through the roof. Margaret was so worn out with sickness and want of sleep she only sat up, and looking round with a weary, bewildered gaze, sunk back on the wet floor. Clara never rose. There was another pause; the ship seemed settling. I clung to Sister Elizabeth, who calmly repeated the 91st Psalm. At length the watch bell rang, and a voice sang out, 'All's well.' Mrs Clarke's voice was now heard above the storm, as she struggled down from her high shelf.

'Stop the ship, stop her pace; the women are all dying with terror; we'll all be dead by the morning, and we must have the doctor.'

So saying, she seized a stool, and brandishing it over my head, struck the roof, saying, 'I tell you, stop the ship; stop her pace.'

Very soon an officer came down to reassure us.

'Poor things,' he said, looking at our disconsolate dripping forms, 'you are in a bad way, but keep up your hearts, the worst is, I hope, over.'

'But,' said Mrs C., 'why don't you stop her pace? Though we do want to go to Scutari, we don't want to be drowned, nor to die of terror.'

'Well, ma'am,' said the officer, 'we are not going so fast now, and there may be reasons you do not know why we should go fast; the captain knows what he is about.'

'Oh! very well,' said Mrs C., appeased; 'we trust to you, only don't let us be drowned.'

'It's not in my power to order the winds and the waves,' he said, 'but we will do all we can for your safety and comfort.'

And he did so by sending down a sailor to swab up the wet and trim our lamp. Soon after the captain himself came down and commiserated us, and said we should be removed to the stern cabin.

The sailor who was employed in swabbing up told us we were running right under the waves, and had nearly sunk, that the water had come in cartloads into the engine-room and put out the fire, and the engine had stopped. He seemed to think there had been real danger, and grumbled at the ship, saying he had never been in a ship so unfit for rough weather, or where the deck was so washed. But the vessel seemed no longer to be cutting through the waves, but rather to be lumbering along at their mercy. Though the danger was evidently far more real than on the former night of alarm, when the nurses were so excited, they seemed now in general too sick, weary, and oppressed to care for danger, and after Mrs C.'s first outcry they were very quiet. I sat beside Sister Elizabeth on a bench all night, wet and cold; but though my railway rug was soaked in sea-water, wet as it was I wrapped it round me, and felt some comfort in it.

At daybreak the captain kindly sent down some strong hot coffee. I now began to be really anxious about some of our sick, they seemed so thoroughly depressed and lifeless. The captain insisted on all who could move going to the stern, where it was dry and comparatively comfortable. I was only too glad to go, and sat there stupefied and exhausted, holding fast, and looking forward to wreck, for the motion continued violent, and I heard repeated crashes.

I sat in this stupid state all day, and in the afternoon, by the surgeon's order, the sick were removed from the wet close cabin to the stern, where we were. But Sister Bertha was faithful to the little hole where she had endured all the discomforts, sickness, and dangers of the voyage, and declined being removed. Sisters Ethelreda and Clara were carried in, miserable beings! I could not help crying when I saw them. I had not seen them for many days (for we could not be said to see one another in that dark cabin), and they were so altered. Sister Ethelreda was gasping, her face ashy white. She looked completely exhausted. We hurriedly made up for her a bed on the table. She had suffered most from want of air, which was not understood by the nurses. One said to me:

'She is always calling for *air*. What does the lady mean? What does she want? Who is air?' (As nobly ignorant of air and its functions as Lord Nelson was, when a child, of fear.)

Clara next appeared; her face was yellow and purple, with a shade of green, suggesting yellow fever. She was still in the wet clothes she had lain in for days. We took them quickly off, and put on her dry ones the stewardess supplied, as we could not get at our own clothes, and we put her in a comparatively comfortable bed on the table, where she soon rallied.

Margaret spent the day on deck, and towards evening she came down and told us some of the cabins next the paddle-box were washed away, and the prow of the ship broken by the violence of the waves, and some fixtures washed away, but that the violence of the storm was abating. The captain ordered room for us to be made in the stern, and we had a quiet night.

3rd November.—We rose about daybreak, and found ourselves near the entrance of the Dardanelles, in sight of the plain of Troy. Miss Nightingale was on deck, looking very worn; the five black dressed nuns were also up. We congratulated each other on getting through our troubles, and drawing near our destination. Some suggested that the siege of Sebastopol might, like that of Troy, last ten years; others thought this impossible, and hoped to hear it had fallen when we reached Scutari. We went quietly through the Dardanelles, stopping a few hours at the castles of Europe and Asia. Here we first saw Turks, little boats full of boys hovered about, and their rough noisy play reminded us of our boys at home, and that boys' nature is somewhat alike all over the world. At nightfall we entered the Sea of Marmora.

4th November.—After a quiet night, we found ourselves

lying, as it were, in the arms of the Queen of the East, in the Golden Horn of the great imperial Constantinople. It was a wet, drizzling morning, but still the beautiful city glittered before us like a dream or a picture. Giddy and confused, we could hardly realise that these painted houses, gay gardens, and glittering minarets were not a vision or panorama. In the afternoon the clouds cleared, and the sun came out, and when we landed, towards evening, the scene was bright and very beautiful. We turned, however, with longing eyes to the ugliest object visible, a great white building opposite Constantinople, which we were told was the Scutari Barracks, where lay our sick and wounded countrymen.

In the evening we crossed the Straits in caiques, four of us in each. They are luxurious conveyances, carved and graceful, the passengers lying on cushions on the bottom, and the picturesque-looking rowers sitting on benches. We thankfully landed at Scutari, which is on the Asiatic side of the Straits, at a little rough pier. Soldiers and a few Turks stood around, and the rough hidès of our men to the poor shrinking Turks, expressed the contempt our men felt for the natives. Our men looked worn and wearied, with pale faces and dirty uniforms, and a few soldiers' wives, too, who were drawn by curiosity to inspect their newly-arrived countrywomen, looked rather wretched and deplorable, weather-beaten and dirty.

We were led up a steep hill to the Barrack Hospital, and directed to Miss Nightingale's quarters, and found her lying exhausted on a couch. Lord Napier, from the Embassy, came in, and welcomed her in a few kind words, to which she answered by thanks. Soon after she recovered sufficiently to take us to our room. The quarters given to her had been occupied by a Russian prisoner—a general, wounded at the Alma—who had died only two days before we arrived.[10] It was in a corner of the great building, which extended over a large space of ground in a quadrangle.

As the building lay on a hill, it was of unequal height, in some parts being only one story high, in other parts it was four.

At each corner was a tower, and corridors ran all round, look-ing towards the inside of the building, the court or rather the field it enclosed, and wards entered from each corridor. The corridors and wards were paved with stone, but very dirty and broken, and round each ward was a raised platform of wood not much more than half a foot high. In each ward was a gallery opposite the window and reached by stairs, very like the galleries in a meeting-house, only they were flat.

On entering the principal or Sultan's gate, we turned to the left, and the tower at the end of this corridor was our quarters. Here, on first entering, was a large room or hall with three large windows, and entering from this on the left was another large room, which Miss N. at once assigned to the nurses; an-other on the right she gave to the ten nuns, a small room or rather closet she kept for herself, and next came a larger room she used as a place of business and for interviews. Some narrow dark stairs between Miss Nightingale's room and the nuns' led to another room in the tower, a fine airy room with windows on three sides, commanding splendid views. Miss N. took us up and said it was to be ours, and we set about at once to clean it, for the dust of ages seemed settled on it. Miss N. sat down with us, and told us the last news from the Crimea, the wonderful charge at Balaclava, and some particulars as to the state of the Hospital.

Soon after she left tea came up in large copper basins—no milk, brown sugar, and stale sour bread, yet never did tea seem more welcome and refreshing.[11] Then came mattresses, sheets, and blankets, such as the soldiers had, marked with the arrow and B.O. [Board of Ordnance.] There was not bedding for us all, so four of us lay without mattresses on the raised divan which, though stuffed with something, was hard as the floor and much rougher, and full of fleas. From this and want of blankets I could not sleep, it seemed very cold. But I was thank-ful to be once more on *terra firma*, and not disposed to grumble.

5th November.—We rose and looked out on this bright Sunday morning on the peaceful-looking, strange, but fair country stretched around. Our room commanded beautiful views in every direction. One set of windows looked over to Constantinople; three others across a plain to the Bosphorus, the General Hospital and adjoining burying ground for our men, the Asiatic Olympus capped with snow in the distance, and the great Mohammedan cemetery; three more commanded a view of a Turkish street facing the entrance to the hospital, a fine mosque, and a distant sweep of the Bosphorus. It was a fine high airy room, and we needed such, as it formed the bed-room, sitting-room, eating-room, chapel—the only place for every purpose for eight women.

After we had opened all the windows and tidied our room, we had breakfast similar to our last night's tea. At first, beyond bedding, we had no furniture in our room, though in time we obtained bedsteads and stools, but to the last no chair or table. The floor was covered with matting, except in the middle, where the rain had destroyed it, and left a large ragged hole which we covered with our boxes, and spread a tablecloth over them at meal-time, and sat round them Turkish fashion, but without the luxury of cushions or mats. We accommodated ourselves to circumstances, and soon began to consider chairs and tables useless luxuries. Indeed at this time we were told there was not a table in the Hospital, even for operations. We had each a tiny brown basin for washing in, a wooden sort of bucket for fetching clean water, a tin pail for removing dirty water.

When there was rain it came into our room, and indeed in heavy rain it used to pour in so that, though we put our whole possessions in the way of basins, pots, pans, and pails to collect it, and emptied each as soon as it filled, we could not prevent their overflowing so as to stream over on the floor and through it into Miss Nightingale's room, and notwithstanding efforts to check its course there it went through to an officer below, who sent up a polite message begging Miss Nightingale and her attendants would refrain from pouring water on him—a natural and innocent request, but one we could not gratify.

The floors are so built that anything spilt descends at once to the room below. One morning I spilt a can of water, and heard it go with a splash into Miss N.'s room. I was so ashamed of this exploit that I did not go down to prayers, but I heard no serious injury was done.

After breakfast we had service below. Mr Sabine, senior chaplain, preached well, but we were longing for work. We had no work appointed as yet, so after dinner we went up into the tower, enjoyed the magnificent prospect, and watched the poor wounded from Balaclava being landed and carried up to the Hospital. How we longed to go and comfort these noble victims to military discipline and courage—the wreck of the six hundred who, at the command of their leader, had ridden without hesitation into the arms of death. But that was not granted us, and we were called on to exercise patience and endurance of inaction this day and on Monday (*6th November*). We tried to console ourselves by making flannel shirts and bandages.

7th November.—On Tuesday, Mr Sabine, the chaplain, asked one of us to go and nurse a dying woman, a soldier's wife, in the last stage of consumption, and I went. He took me to a ward used as a barrack-room, and such a scene of dirt and disorder, rags and tumult it was. Mr S. took me up to the gallery where lay the poor dying woman unnoticed and alone, though the place was covered with beds on the floor miserably dirty, attempts at ragged curtains being put up between them. Some women were lying in child-bed, some rude and noisy, seemingly half-drunk; all dirty, worn out, and squalid-looking, not one bright fresh face to be seen; the very babies were pale and squalid. I remained with my poor woman till nightfall, when a friend came and promised to look after her during the night, and I was ordered to go to our quarters.

8th November.—I went to see after her in the morning, but she was gone, having died in the night. She was already wrapped in a blanket and laid in her grave, the simple inscription 'A Woman' on a piece of wood being put on her grave in the cemetery, where lie peacefully side by side Russians and English, rich and poor. The hopes and joys of many hearts now void and aching lie treasured there by the bright Bosphorus, waiting the morning of the resurrection. Many poor women in that room were widowed that week.

The news of a hard struggle came, but we heard the details first from the lips of the brave men who had witnessed its horrors and suffered in the strife. Before these wounded heroes from Inkerman came in, Miss Nightingale took me and Sister Elizabeth to our appointed work. Dr M'Gregor[12] went with us and took us to the other end of the Hospital, a part called the 'Cholera Wards.' But at this time there was no cholera. All in this division seemed ill of lingering complaints—the results of exposure to damp and cold, fatigue, and bad and insufficient food—low fever, diarrhœa, dysentery, and scurvy. Dr M'Gregor took us round, pointed out the most exhausted, and recommended them to our special care to be attended to and have extra food.[13] He gave us no rule as to the amount or frequency of our supplies, but merely said:

'Give them frequently a little negus or beef-tea—in fact, any simple nourishing thing; they need it.'

And indeed they looked as if they did. One poor fellow looked earnestly at Dr M'Gregor as he gave him to our care, and big tears came rolling silently over his sad wasted face. Dr M'G. spoke kindly and cheeringly to him, but he could not answer but by tears, which seemed to thank him for his kindness, but also to say, 'It comes too late!' And it was too late for him, and for almost all given to us that day. I do not remember any who ultimately recovered, though some lingered long. All we did seemed of no avail, except that at their last hours they had acts and words of kindness which otherwise they had wanted. And were this our only reward, the remembrance of their dying words and looks, their feeble 'God Almighty bless and reward you for all you have done for me,' the knowledge that some of their last hours were soothed by prayer and words of Christ and His eternal love—were this all it pleased God to allow us to do, it were enough to make us glad and thankful.

We went constantly and did what we could, and little as it was, it was deeply appreciated. I used to take a green slop-pail, get it filled with negus, and go round the ward distributing it to those Dr M'G. had entrusted to us; a little later I seized the same green slop-pail, got it filled with beef-tea, and again went round the ward distributing it. We had to pass through crowds of people, Turks and Greeks mending the pavement, soldiers, doctors, and officers. This slop-pail not only did service for me, but was also the vehicle of tea in the afternoon, and performed many other useful offices. But one day it could not be found, and the commotion and distress its absence created was great; and whenever I appeared in that quarter several orderlies ran after me to ask what I had done with the green slop-pail, and as I was quite ignorant of the fate of that useful article I was glad to retreat.

These wards were in a miserable state; there was something more sad and depressing than any other part of the Hospital. The patients were mostly poor fellows whose constitutions had early broken down under hardship; many had never reached the Crimea, very few had seen the battlefield; and they seemed to feel they were dying without glory, that they would not be talked of with the interest and gratitude which was felt for those who had fought and bled. And yet patient, grateful, enduring fellows, unselfish and unexacting, we owed as much to them as to the others—though strength was wanting, the spirit was willing. Deaths were more frequent here than elsewhere; it seemed, indeed, as if our daily lives were spent in the valley of the shadow of death. Daily we missed some pale face we had just learnt to know and love, and who loved us, and daily we watched some solitary pilgrim pass peacefully through the dark waters of death. In the course of a few days all who had been entrusted to us were gone, and were succeeded by others who equally seemed doomed to die.

I used at first always to accompany Sister Elizabeth, who was much beloved by these dying men. Her cheerful, frank, yet gentle manner won their hearts. 'You are like a mother to me,' said a dying lad of nineteen to her within an hour of his death. They all loved her, but she was too anxious, took too much responsibility on herself. She did not care what trouble she took or gave in their service.

At first we did much as we pleased in the ward; Dr M'G., the chief doctor, gave us *carte blanche*. The assistant [Dr D'Arcey] whose immediate duty it was to attend to these men seldom appeared in the wards at all; he was generally smoking in his own quarters. I suppose he felt he could do nothing, and shrunk from witnessing suffering and disease he was unable to relieve. He was soon sent to the Crimea, and two young doctors succeeded him here. One was Maclean of the 42nd [Black Watch]. He was unwearied in his attention to the men, and most devoted to his duty; he examined each case with the most anxious care and attention, and even rose in the night to visit any case he thought precarious. The other did his duty, but in a more routine way. Sister E. being absent, I went with Mr Maclean the first day, and being delighted with his care and kindness to the patients, I went and told her what an exceedingly good young doctor had come. She was vexed to hear of his youth, but was soon reconciled to that, and most thankful for his zeal and devotion. I used to go with the other doctor [Mr Hollingsworth], taking with me a diet-table to put down such extras as he ordered from Miss Nightingale's kitchen. Going round with and taking his directions did not take me much more than half an hour, while Mr Maclean spent hours in going round with Sister Elizabeth, and in examining their patients.

The amount of extras they put down for their men was very much greater—perhaps pudding, wine, and milk for fifty or sixty men. She never could get above half she wished and Mr Maclean ordered, though she always managed to get much more than I did. There was a great difference in the amount of extras we distributed, and I soon observed a corresponding difference in the number of deaths, and was convinced that the careful feeding-up system they pursued did preserve or at least prolong life. This conviction made me very uneasy, for I felt as if my men were dying for want of what I might perhaps by agitating and entreating procure for them. I forget the exact proportion, but I think at the end of a week the deaths in my wards nearly doubled hers, while there was no such difference in the nature of the cases as to account for it. Indeed, the most hopeless cases seemed to be given to Maclean, and the only cause I could see for his losing fewer patients seemed to be his very careful feeding-up system and his careful medical treatment. Sister Elizabeth and I still went together at night. The men were most grateful but gentle and depressed, scarcely speaking but when roused and addressed.

These wards were at this time very unfit for use. The roof let in water; the windows were rickety, and were sometimes blown in on dying men; the broken windows were stuffed with rags—everything looked deplorable and depressing. The doctor wrote requisitions for these evils to be remedied, but in vain. I believe the whole place was found to be in such a ruinous state that to remedy defects in detail was thought useless expense, and it was intended, as soon as the patients could be removed, or were removed by death, to subject the whole to a thorough repair. Meanwhile the poor men lay, as Maclean remarked, in places such as no gentleman would allow any horse he cared for to be stabled. Sometimes when I came in I found all my patients gone—a great blank space being where I left a row of pale faces; but looking round I found them all huddled together in a corner to escape the rain pouring through the roof.

9th November.—The day after we were introduced to our patients, Miss Nightingale sent us to the corridor leading to our quarters, which had hitherto been an empty passage something like the cloisters of a cathedral, but with no architectural beauty, cold, damp, and draughty. Here we found a quantity of straw and sacking made up hastily into beds, and we were desired to sew them up and see them arranged, as wounded patients were immediately expected. So we set to work, Turkish glaziers and carpenters being equally busy, trying hastily to mend defective doors and windows to make this passage more inhabitable. A very tall invalid officer who had been severely wounded and mutilated in an earlier engagement came in a dressing-gown and inspected our preparations.

Just as our beds were made up and arranged on each side of the passage, the patients came in, mostly walking, though their pale faces and severely wounded bodies showed they were scarcely able for this effort. Each was shown his bed, and each without ceremony or delay prepared to occupy it, and we assisted them. Scarcely one was able to undress without assistance; many had lost an arm, others a leg, and all had more or less severe gunshot wounds. In general the men were scrupulously delicate in their conduct, refusing even assistance they needed if it seemed to involve any immodesty, but this day their distress was too great to allow of much consideration of this sort; the one object on their side and on ours was to get them undressed and to bed as quickly as possible, so little nuns were seen hastily but gently pulling off jackets and trousers and unbinding ghastly and revolting wounds which had not been dressed since Sunday, the day on which they had been inflicted, four days since.

The surgeons meanwhile went round examining each wound and giving us directions how to dress them. We had a good supply of warm water, lint, oilskin, and strapping, and each had a basin, so in a short time each patient had not only the comfort of having his stiff and painful wounds dressed, but of a good wash besides, and of a clean shirt—luxuries indeed to men who for weeks had neither the means nor the time to wash themselves or their clothes. It seemed a hard rough place to lie down in, this noisy, windy passage, on a bundle of straw laid on the cold pavement, but to the poor men these hardships seemed luxuries, and they all expressed gratitude and delight. I wish all grumblers could have witnessed that scene, and learnt endurance from these brave men.

On every side we heard our services hailed with delight and gratitude, and some seemed silent only because they felt more deeply. 'This is something like home.' 'This is the first Christian place we've seen many a day.' 'The very sight of a woman does us a world of good, it makes us fancy we've got home to our mothers.' While some shed silent tears, which all their trials, wounds, and hardships had not had power to bring. When all were settled quietly in bed, soup was brought in and administered, Mrs Clarke being distributor-in-chief, and telling each who received it how much less he needed it than others, how thankful he ought to be, &c, &c.

But after this day I had no further intercourse with these Inkerman heroes. Miss Langston, H. Erskine, and Margaret attended to the wounded. Sister Elizabeth and I continued to attend the sick first entrusted to us. But this day's intercourse gave me an idea of the battle more fearful and vivid than any written detail could give. We read its horrors in the wounds, and still more in their words and manner. They all seemed to think that but for the French it would have been a defeat; not that our men could or would have yielded, but that they would have been annihilated, crushed by overwhelming numbers. 'Och! there's too many of them for us entirely! there's no end of them,' said one poor fellow.

All expressed a grateful, generous admiration of our brave allies. 'They're true brothers, and alongside of us they'll do anything.' There seemed a general opinion that the Russians were drunk, to which our poor men attributed their cruelty in stabbing the wounded, and their brutality when wounded in attacking those who came to offer them assistance as they lay.

10th November.[14]—We passed through these newly arrived wounded patients, who seemed for the most part doing well, and went to our dreary wards to wait on our more silent suffering sick. Patient, gentle, noble sufferers, not one rude unseemly word was heard; they seemed like worn-out children sinking to rest; languid, and already almost dead to everything, except when their eyes brightened with love and gratitude as they recognised Sister Elizabeth, and stretched out their wasted hands and arms to express the thanks they were too feeble to utter. It was a harrowing thought to remember the wives and mothers at home, whose eyes would never rest on these beloved forms, who were now waiting with anxious beating hearts, soon to be wrung out and made desolate for life. The one thought that seemed most deeply graven on the hearts of these dying men was the remembrance of their mother's love. Their gratitude to us was expressed by it 'like a mother.'

One Scotch lad, sending a message by me to his mother, said, 'Tell her I'll think on her all night, for I know she's thinking on me.' Again he said, 'I hope I may yet return to be a comfort to her in her auld age.' He died that very night. No doubt his last thoughts were with his mother, who survived him above thirty years.

One night, as Sister Elizabeth and I were returning through a long dark corridor, we met a tall soldier staggering along as if unable to walk, bent down, and actually crying like a child. We spoke to him, and found that he had landed that night with a number of sick, but not being able to keep up with the others, had fallen behind, lost his way, and now knew not where to lay his weary aching limbs. We took him from ward to ward till we found an empty bed. On returning to our quarters, we found ourselves shut out, as the nurses had retired to rest. However, on our ringing, Miss Nightingale herself opened the door, and on hearing our story, she searched out some provisions and sent us back with them to our poor exhausted friend, and remained up to let us in on our return. She looked, I thought, very sweet and kind, though delicate and worn out. About this time Sister Ethelreda, who had never recovered from the voyage, and could not eat the food,[15] was sent home.

One night, some hours after we had gone to bed, Mrs Clarke knocked at our door, and asked if one of us would rise and go to a poor dying man, who earnestly asked for some one to pray with him. Mrs C. said: 'I inquired into his religion. If he had been a Roman Catholic I would have asked a nun to go, but being Church of England, I thought best to come to you, as I fancy you are more up to that sort of thing than the nurses.' Miss Langston dressed quickly, went, and remained with him most of the night.

I sometimes longed for a little change, to see some rally and recover, to help to restore some to their friends and country, for all we seemed able to do for our poor sick, seemed to be merely to cheer and prolong their dying hours. Very few would return to England, and if any survived to return, their constitutions were ruined; a few months had done the work of years—in mind, character, and constitution they were aged men, though in years they were but boys.

One day, one of the nurses who attended the wounded in the General Hospital being sick, Miss N. sent me in her place. I found this most interesting, though very different work. The men were lively and cheerful, mostly recovering, merry, light-hearted, joking on their wounds and losses. They looked forward to a speedy return to their home and country, and felt they had done their duty, and that family and nation would receive them gladly and gratefully. Their strife and sufferings were nearly over. Life, hope, and happiness lay before them. Though for the most part maimed and disabled, they felt their Queen and country would acknowledge their self-sacrifice, and be proud of them. A few, though but a few, looked forward to return to their brave comrades before Sebastopol, and to share yet more sufferings and more dangers, and not one seemed to shrink from it; a few were in too great anguish to look beyond the present, and a few were dying.

One poor dying fellow, called Nicols, seemed to be neglected by the orderlies *because* he was dying. He was very dirty, covered with wounds, and devoured by lice. I pointed this out to the orderlies, whose only excuse was—'It's not worth while to clean him; he's not long for this world.' I washed his face and hands, cut away his hair, and tried to make him a little less uncomfortable, and he was so grateful, he would scarcely let me leave him. His eyes were inflamed, and I gave him a little soft cambric rag for them, as he injured them by rubbing them with his dirty hands; in fact, by conveying bad matter from his wounds to his eyes and face, they had got into a fearfully painful state. His flannel shirt was dark, and seemed moving with lice, it stuck into his bed-sores; he needed a woman's constant care, but I was unable to return to him. I hope some one soothed his dying hours, and that he did not look and call for me in vain. The men in bed on each side of him, helpless themselves, looked on him with pity, and told me his state was such that lice swarmed from him to them.

During the forenoon I was busily engaged in unbinding and washing wounds for the doctor's inspection, then in dressing them by his direction. In the afternoon I read and talked to some, and wrote for others. It was interesting to hear their individual tales of the dark days of Balaclava and of Inkerman. One poor Irishman told me how he fell wounded, and tried to crawl under a bush at Inkerman, and how the Russians, passing by, struck at and stabbed him again and again, grinning at him between each stab.

'God forgive me for judging them,' he said, 'but surely they are no true Christians.'

He opened his shirt and showed the wounds and stabs they had inflicted. They then knocked him on the head till he was stunned and insensible. But he revived even after this treatment, and lay quiet, fearing if he gave signs of life he would be murdered outright. Then he had the pleasure of hearing the French come and charge over him, he said:

'I thought they would have trodden me to death, but I did not mind that. Och! it was grand! It would have done your heart good to hear the shout we raised as they came alongside of us and drove back the enemy.'

I suppose it did his heart good, poor fellow, for the state of the wounded as they lay in suffering and expecting a cruel murderous death was the most trying of all they went through. Some told me no words could express the anguish of these hours, as they lay helpless, inactive, waiting to be murdered, as too many were in cold blood, or rather in drunken brutality. One poor fellow, an Irish dragoon, had been wounded in the Balaclava charge—very severe wounds in arm, thigh, and leg. I never saw wounds more fearful-looking and offensive. His face bore an expression of deep anguish, though he neither groaned nor cried. When I first came he looked anxiously about, saying: 'Would to God some one would come and do my arm.'

I said, 'Let me do it.'

'Oh no,' he answered, 'you could never bear the sight nor the smell.'

However, when the doctor came, he asked me to unbind and wash it, then he came himself to examine, burn, and dress it. His wounds were severe and painful, but I hope not fatal.

The General Hospital in which these cases lay was about half a mile from the Barracks, in a sort of plain or common on which our army encamped when it first landed, and which still bore marks of the tents. Several of the men said to me:

'Ah, if we had gone on straight to Sebastopol instead of staying here, dancing and amusing ourselves, it might have been all over by this time, and more of us left to rest and amuse ourselves. Few of us who danced here on the Queen's last birthday and drank her health are above ground now, and those few are in a sorry way.'

The General Hospital is built on the same plan as the Barracks, but not above one quarter the size. It was generally used as a Turkish Military Hospital, and when our army first arrived, was occupied by the surviving victims of the Sinope massacre. It was cleaner and less gloomy than the Barracks, and was at this time devoted to the wounded, who were in a much more cheerful, hopeful state of mind than the poor sick. It was also a much less gloomy building. The interior square was occupied by a garden, and the patients who could walk used to go there and fetch flowers for their bedridden comrades. The first day I went there I found almost every patient confined to bed had a rose lying beside him. No ladies nor nurses lived at this time in the General Hospital, but Miss N. sent a party there every morning to help in dressing wounds, and in the afternoon the sisters went to read or write for the patients.

About ten days after we arrived, we were roused and kept awake by a most violent storm. Being in a tower, we were much exposed to its violence, and the noise was fearful, howling, whistling, and rattling. The windows in the room above us were blown in, as they were in various parts of the building. It was this night the *Prince*, laden with valuable stores of every description and every comfort for our men, went down at Balaclava with twenty-one other vessels. On hearing of these disasters we all felt disheartened, and dreaded the coming winter, and day by day we saw deeper cause and proof of distress.

Though the Hospitals gradually improved in every way, the number of patients rapidly increased, and the state in which they arrived became daily more hopeless and depressing. Daily we saw men carried in whose state of filth no words can describe, and with death written on their discoloured faces, it was heart-rending to see their imploring countenances as they were carried from ward to ward seeking in vain a place to lie down in. They seemed to entreat to be laid down anywhere to die in peace. I have seen their sad eyes look imploring at the orderlies, as if to say, 'For pity's sake let me rest here;' while the orderlies, hardened and hurried, answered:

'What do you bring him here for? We have no room, be off! We don't want any more of his sort here, we have more already than we can look to.'

Then the bearers would raise the poor sufferer with a hasty jerk, saying: 'What are we to do with him? We cannot keep walking round the hospital with him all day.' And at last they would insist on laying down their sad burden in some empty space from which a corpse had just been removed, amidst the grumbling of the orderlies whose duty it was to receive and nurse him.

It may seem such conduct in the orderlies, considering that they were fellow-soldiers of the poor sufferers, was most un-feeling and inconsistent with the general character of the sol-diers, and certainly all orderlies were not selfish and heartless, but on the whole they seemed to me very inferior in character to the other soldiers. I think the finer and nobler men scorned the inactivity and safety of hospital life, and preferred much the dangers and hardships of the camp before Sebastopol to such women's work as nursing and sweeping, so that they were rather the dregs of the army who became orderlies, and their motive being selfish safety, they had no real love for their duty.

Speaking of their hardness and neglect, one of my best and bravest patients said to me:

'I can't blame them, for I have no patience myself with sick men calling out like helpless babies for this thing and that thing. I believe if I were orderly, I'd knock half of them over the head, and get rid of them.'

And yet this patient was suffering severe and prolonged ill-ness, and was a man of warm kind feelings. Indeed it seems an unnatural occupation for men, especially for young lads, to have the care of sick and dying men. And it is either unduly depressing or hardening and demoralising for the wild buoy-ancy of youth to be thrust into such scenes. I have seen lads frolicking about by the bedside of their dying comrades, caught them even at leap-frog along the feet of a row of suf-ferers, some in anguish, some in the awful stillness of death; and if reproved, 'We can do them no good, poor fellows; we must keep up our own spirits a bit,' was the answer.

I have seen men I thought well of as patients, on recovering and being made orderlies, show a negligence, hardness, and indifference that surprised me, and I scarcely knew an orderly who could get leave to go out and come in sober. They had great excuse; they were confined day and night to the pes-tilential air of the sick wards; they had to perform offices for the dead and dying much more trying than any we had to do;

they *were expected*, in addition to their day's work, to sit up every third night (though few if any performed this duty). They mostly lay down in their clothes, and slept so soundly no cries from those who needed their help could rouse them. One dear fellow told me the poor man next him, who was dying, called repeatedly in much distress for the orderly, but in vain, and that he too shouted as loudly as he could in behalf of his poor distressed comrade, but their united cries could not rouse the orderly, and neither having strength to move or stand, they called till they grew hoarse, and lost power even to call. This, I believe, often happened.

Some old pensioners sent out as orderlies[16] did no better, in one respect worse, for their health universally gave way, and they soon became patients. One of these in the ward I served was absurdly angry with himself for having got into this scrape.

'What in the world possessed me,' he said, 'to volunteer like a fool to come out here and ruin my constitution this way? Could I not be content to be comfortable at home, and not volunteer like a fool?'

'Don't call yourself a fool,' I said, 'you volunteered like a brave old man.'

'Nay,' he answered, 'more like a brave old jackass.'

I do think one great use of the nurses was their influence on the orderlies in checking their carelessness and roughness, in encouraging, cheering, and directing the more attentive and kind-hearted, and in watching that the very weak were not neglected. I did see neglect in those parts where there was no woman which no nurse would have allowed, and which the doctors who went through the wards, but did not remain in them, were not cognisant of. Some of the orderlies seemed quite as cheered and pleased with the presence of nurses as the poor patients themselves, especially in those depressed and depressing sick wards. One especially (whom we called the Flamingo, from his brilliant red hair, moustache, and beard, which hung down over his chest) used to watch for us with anxiety, and introduce us to the cases he thought required most attention. But in general, I think, the orderlies felt themselves degraded at being in the comparative safety and comfort of the Hospital, instead of sharing the dangers and hardships of their comrades before Sebastopol. The patients who had any hope of recovery all looked eagerly forward to return to their regiment, and to share its hardship, dangers, and glory.

I fear dishonesty was not uncommon among the orderlies, and there were considerable facilities and temptations, as the poor men had frequently a little money about their person, which the orderly who waited on them knew of, and could easily remove from the dead or dying. The extreme confusion there seemed to be in every department offered temptations to dishonesty. One patient took 2s. 6d. out of his purse to reward an orderly for his services. The orderly, seeing gold in the purse, seized it, and when the patient resisted, killed him with one blow on the head. He was seized, tried, and hung. He had been a thief, and the sight of gold maddened him.

About the beginning of December a few cases of Asiatic cholera occurred.[17] The first were of two young men about twenty, who were taken ill together. One was servant of Colonel W. This lad seemed in great terror, and kept recalling the most awful parts of Scripture, those of anger and judgement, especially from the first chapter of Proverbs. He recovered. The other seemed more composed, and calmly prepared for death. He was on the eve of his twenty-first birthday, and was anxious to live to that day that he might leave a little money (£60) which then became his to a sister he was fond of, but he died an hour before. He had been at Alma, and having a facility for versifying, had made a poem describing that battle, which he recited at intervals this last evening of his life. What was stranger, he made and repeated verses on the cholera, descriptive of his present sufferings, which he seemed to feel were only to end in death. His last words were, 'I dread the sufferings of this night.' A few minutes afterwards they were over.

We had had some experience of cholera in Plymouth and Devonport in the summer and autumn of 1849, and also during a slighter outbreak in 1852, and so we were generally sent to the few cases of cholera which now occurred. Most of them were fatal. They were put under the charge of that devoted young surgeon, Maclean of the 42nd, and he did his duty nobly, patiently, and unweariedly. But he complained, as it seemed to me justly, of having patients removed from other parts of the Hospital to his care when almost at the point of death. This occurred repeatedly, and one night on going his rounds he found a new patient just introduced from another ward completely exhausted, unable to speak, in fact dying. At that moment Dr M. [Menzies], his superior officer, passed, and Maclean went up to him and remonstrated reasonably, and, as it seemed to me, very respectfully on the subject.

He said: 'I cannot possibly treat men of whose illness I can only judge by the last symptoms. If anything can be done for them, surely it is best done by the medical man who has attended them during the earlier stages of their illness. It is merely disturbing them at their last moments, and destroying any hope of their recovery, to remove them in this state, while at the same time it is unjust to me and injurious to my patients to have men brought in merely to die among them.'

Dr M. answered shortly, it could not be helped; but he went with Miss Nightingale, who was with him, to see this dying man, and finding that he was rapidly sinking, he seemed irritated, and used such rough words to Mr Maclean that he left the ward without answering, while Miss N. sent me and Sister Elizabeth for hot water and brandy.

The nurses being at evening prayers (10 P.M.), there was a little delay in getting what was wanted, so that Dr M. and Miss N. followed us, and while Miss N. procured it Sister Elizabeth defended Mr Maclean's conduct to Dr M., and spoke of his zeal and devotion. Dr M. seemed angry unreasonably, though he was in general kind; but I often observed that the kindest and most zealous doctors sometimes seemed exasperated by the death of their patients, and vented their disappointment and vexation on any one who came in their way. I found this so much the case subsequently that, in the General Hospital, I avoided my doctor as much as possible when any patient he was interested in was dying. But to return to the present case, we brought the hot bottles and brandy, and Miss N. asked me to rub his feet while she gave him brandy, but she soon desisted, for he was dying, and in a few minutes he breathed his last. This was in a small ward containing eight or ten beds, and during the next day all the patients in it except two died. Mr Maclean dreaded the effect of death in depressing the survivors, so when this poor stranger died first, he asked us to remain in the ward, and attend to the other patients, standing so as to prevent their seeing their poor companion removed, which we did.

Miss Nightingale afterwards went with Mr Maclean into the deadhouse, where above ten who had died that day lay. It was an awful place to visit at any time, and as I waited at the door and saw her calmly uncover the faces of the dead, and look on them as they lay far from wife or mother in that dreary place, it seemed strange to see one so frail, graceful, and refined standing at the dead of night alone amid such sad scenes of mortality.

One of the poor men who died in this ward next day was a Scotchman. He seemed to suffer more intense agony than others (for in general they seemed without suffering at the last), but the expression of this man's face, and his cries, denoted extreme pain. Another in the next bed, also dying, seemed to feel for his poor comrade, though his mind was wandering. He stretched out his feeble hand to stroke him, and kept saying, 'Poor fellow, are you better now?'

Next evening, as Sister Elizabeth and I visited this ward, we found it deserted; the orderly whose duty it was to attend had been included in Dr M.'s displeasure the night before, and choosing to console himself by drinking, was absent, and the men lay alone quietly dying, a dim lamp burning. The poor

Scotch soldier's violent agonies were over; he lay raised up in bed with open mouth and glazed eyes fixed on the light. Sister E., thinking him dying, hurriedly asked me to remain while she went for Miss Nightingale, who was particularly interested in these men. When she left, I went up to him and spoke to him; he did not move or answer. I touched him, and found he was dead, though still warm and flexible. Finding life gone, I laid him down, closed his eyes and mouth, and straightened his limbs.

About this time, the end of November, Miss Nightingale took me with her one night to distribute shirts to Sister Elizabeth's patients. All to whom she gave shirts were without any, and she asked each what had become of his. Some said they had worn theirs till it was so filthy and full of lice they had to take them off and have them burnt; others told us they had taken them off and given them to comrades who had none, and were ordered to get up, and therefore needed them more than those still in bed. This seemed true charity, such as few are called to exercise.

Miss N. gave me directions for myself, and especially for Sister Elizabeth, as her zeal and energy on behalf of her men were getting rather troublesome. She got such large requisitions from Mr Maclean on Miss Nightingale's kitchen that it was found impossible to supply them, and Miss Nightingale requested them, in justice to the rest of the Hospital, to make smaller requisitions.

One day Mr Maclean ordered pudding for forty men, and as only three puddings were made, of course this large demand could not be met. The eldest nun, generally called the Rev. Mother, who had the charge of the food, gave us as much as she could afford for Sister E., which I took to her; but Sister E. told me to take it away, as it would only tantalise the men to give them a spoonful each, or to give it to some and not to others. However, I thought a mouthful better than nothing, and was about to distribute it, when the Rev. Mother came in with a little more she had obtained, and offered it; but Sister E.

met her, and declined what she brought, at the same time begging her not to trouble herself to come to these wards. In fact, Sister E. was hurt and irritated at her patients being disappointed of their pudding, so that the brave fellows themselves tried to comfort her by telling her 'not to mind or vex herself, better days were coming.' The Rev. Mother and Mrs C. had conjointly the distribution of food from Miss N.'s kitchen, and I always tried to get my allowance from the nun, who was ever patient, calm, and attentive to every request. However these nuns may have erred in faith and practice, the deepest impression their conduct left was one of affectionate admiration; their invariably patient, cheerful, gentle manners, their constant, considerate kindness, left a very pleasing remembrance, a beautiful picture of true and practical Christianity, which those who boast a purer faith would do well to emulate.

Sister Elizabeth appealed to Miss Nightingale as to the pudding, who promised more for the next day; at the same time, she repeated her advice to ask the doctor to give less liberal orders, as such demands were unfair to the other wards. Next day the promised pudding was not forthcoming; and so there went on a daily contention for food, Mr Maclean and Sister E. striving to get more for their men than the Rev. Mother and Mrs C. could give, Mrs C. scolding Sister E. for asking so much, and Sister E. getting excited and anxious. I generally got all my doctor ordered for my men, and this was very much less than Sister E.'s share; and I sometimes feared that had my men more nourishment their lives might have been prolonged, but as no effort on my part could have procured more, though unhappy, my conscience was easy.

About the beginning of December Miss Nightingale told me she would change my work, and send me to the General Hospital. Though for some reasons glad of the change, I was sorry to be separated from Sister E., who remained at the Barracks, and for some time she had little to do, as the wards which we had attended were broken up, the remaining patients being distributed through the Hospital while the wards underwent repairs, which they greatly needed. The Turkish carpenters and glaziers seem to do their work fairly, and to have great strength, though they lived poorly. They frequently cut their hands at their work, and used with trusting simplicity to show their small wounds as we passed, and by signs ask our assistance in healing them. Of course, when so appealed to, we were glad of the opportunity of showing kindness to the poor fellows, and thankful for the trusting respect they showed to us, whom they might be expected to despise doubly as giaours [infidels], and as women. But we never experienced from man, woman, or child anything but respect and kindness. 'Boonie Johnnie' was the term bestowed on us without distinction. The Turks themselves were universally addressed as 'Johnnie,' and in their turn they applied this term to us as well as to the soldiers. 'Boonie' or 'bono' expressed approbation; 'no bono' the reverse. One day a little Spanish boy addressed us, and in a broken mixture of languages he told us he came from Spain, and had seen both Liverpool and London. He was polite and pleasing; he said, 'Englis bono, Turk bono; Greek no bono, no bono.'

Our men often reproached the poor Turks—'Ah, Johnnie, no bono! Johnnie hidès Balaclava'—meaning to refer to the disastrous cowardice of that day. I said to one of my patients, as he said this:

'I suppose the officers ran, and the poor men could not stand alone. What would you do if your officers ran away?'

He laughed at the idea, and said, 'Faith, if my officers ever so forgot themselves, I think I would make the best of my way after them.'

Till January we continued to live or rather to sleep in the tower. After breakfast we set out to walk to the General Hospital together, walking, except four who went in a carriage which came every day to carry the weak or lazy nurses. Two nuns generally headed this party, Sister Mary de Gonzaga and Sister Jean de Chantal. Both these nuns were very nice-looking. Sister Mary was very pale, with large expressive grey eyes; Sister Jean was very rosy, and had bright black eyes. Eight or ten nurses went, and three of our party—Sisters Bertha, Margaret, and myself. It was a beautiful walk (though rather rough, and in wet weather difficult from the mud), across a plain or common commanding a beautiful view of the Bosphorus and Constantinople and the British and Turkish burying-grounds. There was an inlet of the sea which looked like an inland lake surrounded by hills, the more distant capped with snow, which often suggested to us the Sea of Galilee. A little north-east of Constantinople lay a beautiful village on the coast. Turkish towns in the distance have a peculiarly brilliant appearance, but a nearer inspection generally disappoints, from the dirty, untidy habits of the inhabitants. I think this village is called Cadinople, from the number of Cadis who live there.

The carriage which conveyed some of the nurses was ornamentally carved and gilt, like the old pictures of the Lord Mayor's coach. It was certainly more elegant than a London cab, but not so convenient or well hung; indeed it seemed infirm and shaky. It had no door; we had, as it were, to step over a pretended low door and insert ourselves through the window, which at first some of us felt a puzzling operation. One nurse attempted it several times, but putting in her head first, found it impossible to make her feet follow. Being told she must put one foot in, then stoop and get in her head, she said, 'No, I'll never go in foot foremost,' and gave it up in despair. It was still more awkward to descend, as we had to put out one foot first; it had somewhat the effect of scrambling foot foremost out of a carriage window, and was seldom effected with dignity and decorum.

One day, when our carriage arrived, and the nurses began to appear foot foremost out of the window, Dr O'Flaherty ran forward and attempted to open the door, fancying it was overzeal led them to disembark in that fashion; but he soon found his polite efforts vain, as there was no real door to open. I avoided this carriage as much as possible, preferring the bracing beautiful walk, though I was sometimes forced to go, as a nun or sister was expected to go in each carriage. When condemned to this vehicle, I got so cross that Margaret good-humouredly admonished me to submit to my fate with the resignation of a Christian. I generally preferred to make my exit at the outside window, and to land unseen in the mud, rather than to do so in the midst of the doctors and officers who generally stood about the Hospital door. Though I do not think it was above half a mile, it seemed quite a journey; we jolted along so slowly and with such effort, and at half-way the driver got down, unharnessed his horse, and led him away to be watered, leaving us to conjecture whether he meant to return or not. The road was so wet at times that one day a gentleman returning to the Barracks asked Sister Mary if he could do anything there for her or fetch anything.

She said, laughing, 'I wish you could send us a boat to take us back to the Barracks.'

'Ah,' he answered, 'I wish you could send me a boat to take me back to England.' This gentleman very soon after was seized with cholera and died; his wife died also within a few days of the same terrible disease.

The General Hospital had a very different aspect from the Barracks; it seemed cleaner, lighter, and more cheerful in every way. The wards were in better repair; no broken window stuffed with rags, no rain streaming in, no beds on the floor—everything in better order. The men, too, were very much more cheerful; they were when I first went mostly wounded from Alma, Balaclava, and Inkerman, and mostly recovering. Sister M. de Gonzaga, who seemed to have a sort of general charge of the nurses here, showed me my division, which was half of D Corridor and two adjoining wards, and introduced me to an orderly, who on the doctor's entrance presented me as the nurse. He was a little man, quick in perception, and rather so in temper. He gave me directions as to washing the wounds and dressing the slighter ones, forbidding rather needlessly the use of a sponge.[18] I used a bit of tow, and of course burnt it, and took a fresh bit after each wound. There was a good supply of warm water, and I emptied and rinsed out my basin every time it was used.

The men rejoiced to have a nurse, and told me I was much cleaner and gentler than the orderly, who used, when the doctor was engaged, to wash several patients' wounds in the same water. I began operations on a fearfully filthy and shattered leg of an Alma Irishman, who shouted out, 'Och! the blessing of the touch of a woman's hand; she touches my poor leg so tinder and gentle!' Of course men whose hands were hard and horny through labour—hands used once perhaps to the plough, and more recently to the firelock—were not fitted to touch, bathe, and dress wounded limbs, however gentle and considerate their hearts might be.

It seemed to us a mistake to think that because these sick and wounded men were soldiers they should be roughly treated, and denied comforts in weakness and suffering. Some seemed to dread the ladies and nurses coddling and spoiling the men; but really, however much they might be inclined to do so, in our circumstances we had not the means—our utmost efforts could not procure common comforts nor put our patients at all on a level with those in an English workhouse or infirmary. Besides, sickness, like death, is a great leveller—the same remedies, and in a great measure the same comforts, are fitted for all ranks. Wounds, diarrhœa, and fever know no distinctions of rank.

One doctor said to Margaret rather contemptuously, as she passed him with a dish of jelly in her hands (which was sent regularly by Lady Stratford Canning[19]), 'Calves' foot jelly for soldiers!'

'For dying men,' she answered.

'Well,' he said, 'since you've got it, I will show you a case or two in which it may be useful.'

But to return to my own wards and my own men. Murphy, the rosy-cheeked Irishman who had rejoiced so in the touch of a woman's hand, told me his leg had had no chance till I took it in hand, the orderlies were so rough and careless that their washing did more harm than good. He said for long it was untouched, and swarmed with maggots. Many were the blessings this fine old fellow showered on me day by day. (I call him old, for many were but lads, and he had served sixteen years, and so was considered an old soldier—he was thirty-three.)

Leaving him, I passed on from wound to wound, and spent the whole morning washing and dressing them. One poor lad, fearfully emaciated, sat up on his bed leaning on an orderly (for he was too weak to sit unsupported), and looking with great, sad, wistful eyes on me. I heard him ask the orderly to get me to do his arm. I was at once attracted by his look and voice, and went to him and uncovered his wound. It was the right arm taken out of the socket, and an abscess formed beneath; he had also a slighter wound and fearful bedsores more painful than his arm, and he was so wasted—his bones in every part seemed cutting through the skin. He was of the 1st Royals, and when his regiment and the Greys were trying to cover the retreat of the Light Cavalry, a cannon ball took off his arm. He had been slightly wounded in the earlier charge, but refused to retire and have it attended to. He told me he only felt a shock and did not know what had happened till he looked down and saw his arm hanging, when he rode off as well as he could to where the surgeons were operating. On the road he would have fallen off had a comrade not held him on and encouraged him.

At last he reached where the wounded were being treated, and some bluejackets lifted him tenderly from his horse and carried him into a hut. He told me that, faint and suffering as he was, they made him laugh, as they lifted him, by their nautical talk—'Unship this poor fellow—loose that tackling there;' and then a great strong fellow took him as if he were a baby and carried him into a back room—the front being full of wounded. There he lay, lonely and faint from loss of blood, till a surgeon came and examined his wound. He immediately called another surgeon, who said he could not come, being engaged with some officers. The first, who seemed a senior officer, said, 'I desire you to come at once; this lad's life depends on immediate attention.' So they came and took off his right arm out of the socket. No chloroform was used, but they gave him some rum, and in an hour he was lying on board ship, where he spent days on the bare boards often wet, so that when he reached Scutari the skin of his back was much broken producing very painful bedsores.

He was a gentle lad, very sensitive, though lively and full of spirit. He had been brought up by an indulgent grandmother, of whom he told me I reminded him. He said one reason he enlisted was that being apprenticed in London, he was so unhappy, and so missed his grannie and his home, that he could not bear it, so he enlisted, and found, poor boy, a rough grandmother in the service and in the battlefield. But he had not, like some, enlisted in haste and repented at leisure; he loved his calling, and never repented having enlisted. It was a long-formed plan; he waited patiently till he was tall enough, though he kept his intention secret for fear of opposition. He went down to the country to visit his grandparents, but would not grieve them by telling his intentions. On returning he enlisted, and next day joined his regiment at Manchester. This was in October 1853. When not long after the regiment was ordered abroad, being but a recruit he might have stayed at home, but he volunteered to go, and was sent. He was only sixteen, but a fine, tall, handsome, broad-chested lad, with a beautiful, interesting face. When I first saw him there was something inexpressibly touching in his timid desponding air, his very expressive large eyes so often filled with tears, his extreme weakness, and the severe pain he suffered, his gentleness and grateful attachment, and in the midst of all and above all his generous anxiety for and interest in his fellow-sufferers, made him the object of peculiar regard. The anxiety as to his recovery—as his life for weeks seemed trembling in the balance—increased the interest he created. Besides, amiable as he was—gentle, affectionate, and unselfish—he seemed afraid to die; he was ignorant of the truths of the Gospel, and the power of faith in Christ; he was not prepared to die, and this made me doubly anxious for his recovery. When this gentle boy shed tears from anguish and weakness of his hard bed, ridiculed for this weakness by his harder and rougher companions; grumbled at often by the orderlies for giving the trouble his weak and helpless state exacted; it created a sympathy and anxiety no words can express. Thanks be to God, he was restored, and may He grant it be not only to his friends and country, but to his Heavenly Father, his Redeemer, his home above.

At the other end of my division lay an Irishman—old Tom Burns—with a most fearfully shattered leg from Inkerman, which the doctor had condemned for amputation, and accordingly it lay undressed and untouched on the bare rough sacking, caked in blood and matter, with deep putrid holes. The possessor of this leg was a fine old veteran of thirty-three, but with worn, weather-beaten marks of age on him, his hair thin and grey, his handsome spirited face withered and lined. His ever ready joke and merry ringing laugh were the only signs of youth about him.

'God bless you,' he said, as I took in hand his poor neglected leg, washed and dressed it. 'God bless you, and if I save my leg, it will be your doing.'

Next day he maintained that it was better, and that the touch of my hand had given it a turn, and that he would always say so. The doctor had said that nothing could be done for it; it must come off. But Dr O'Flaherty said, 'It is a desperate case, but as he seems to have a good healthy constitution, we'll leave it on a few days and see.' The other doctor rather pressed its immediate amputation, and said he could do no more for it. Still Dr O'Flaherty gave it a week's respite, and it was during this week I got possession of it, as the doctor left it alone, and did not even look at it. As the day fixed for the operation came on, the doctor came to examine it, and finding it decidedly improving, it was left on. The poor man seemed quite indifferent on the subject, perfectly contented to rest on the doctor's decision as to whether his leg was to be off or on.

Murphy, the Alma-wounded Irishman, had a decided inclination to get rid of his. 'It will never be any good,' he used to say; 'shure, doctor dear, you threw away many a better leg at the Alma; I'll thank you to take it off.'

I think it was seeing stumps heal much faster than his poor leg, the being condemned for an indefinite time to lie on his back watching the slow and often retrograde progress of his wound, as bit after bit of shattered bone worked out, and also knowing that the loss of a limb would ensure him a better pension. All this, I think, led him to long for amputation. But the amputations which took place in the hospital were, as far as I knew, mostly unsuccessful. The patient sunk and died under the operation, or soon after it; while those amputated on the field mostly recovered. The reason of this was, I think, that on the field the men were in the full vigour of life, and able to bear the pain and exhaustion, while those operated on in the hospital were almost invariably men whose constitutions were worn out with suffering, every effort having been made to preserve the limb, and amputation being only employed as a last resort when the powers of life were at a low ebb.

Tom Burns' buoyant spirits very much tended to his recovery. Laughing seems as conducive to health as sighing is the reverse; and Tom not only kept his lungs in good play by laughing and joking, but also benefited all his fellow-sufferers within his reach, for he would not let them mope or despond; and I have often seen one inclined to do so cheered and almost forced to laugh at his pleasant amusing talk. With all his fun he was never guilty of the slightest impropriety or irreverence. There was nothing in his fun to offend delicacy or religion. He was a married man and an affectionate husband. He could read, and said the books he cared most for were the Bible— and *Punch*.

He used to say to the orderlies when they lifted him, 'Take care of me for the sake of the ould woman that owns me.' I thought that was his mother, but found she was his wife, and only twenty-eight. As he could not write, I wrote to her for him, and in course of time he received an answer worthy of him and of Ireland, full of the warmest sympathy and affection, and yet with a vein of fun and humour running through it. Tom was, I believe, sincerely religious, a Roman Catholic, but not bigoted. He was fond of reading the New Testament. I fear his temptation in health would be drink. When I first attended him he had daily a good allowance of port wine, which he saved up for several days. However, the doctor discovered this, and ordered it to be taken from him. In desperation he seized and drank the whole at once. Consequently he got into such an excited state that, not knowing the circumstances, I feared derangement, he talked so wildly, and seizing his poor shattered leg he threatened to throw it out of the window.

Next day he was thoroughly sober and ashamed of this outbreak. His wine was quite stopped from this time, and he submitted with good humour to this deprivation. He only asked me to take the cradle off his legs, saying, 'As the doctors think fit to wean their baby, and take his bottle from him, I think he ought to be getting out of his cradle, and hope he'll soon run alone.'

There were three legs in a similar state in this corridor—the two Irish ones, Burns and Murphy, and between them an English one, wounded at Balaclava. The Englishman (whose name I forget) was quiet, grave, and well-behaved. They used to compare legs every morning, and often to conjecture which would first be ready for service. Burns' was at first far the most desperate, but when it began to amend it improved more rapidly than the others. So Burns said he was determined to be not much behind the others, if he did not get up first and pull them out of bed. However the Englishman first received permission to rise, and he rather crowed over poor Burns as he put on his hospital dressing-gown. The same evening, as I passed by, one of the patients sitting by the stove rose and said in a triumphant tone, 'Good evening, ma'am.' I was puzzled, but immediately recognised Tom's merry laugh which followed, and found that as soon as his English fellow-sufferer had gone back to bed, Tom had got hold of his dressing-gown, managed to put it on, got up without leave, and hobbled to the fire, where he sat laughing and joking in full force. I remonstrated, and advised his immediate return to bed, which he promised should take place as soon as I left. Sometimes he amused himself by decking his poor shattered leg with roses, and lay admiring it.

One evening the doctor, after probing it, put in the forceps and tried in vain to bring out a piece of bone, Tom looking on with a most stoic expression. After some attempts, the doctor gave it up, first asking Tom 'if he felt it?'

'Not a bit,' said Tom.

The moment after the doctor went hastily away, and as I wiped away the blood and matter flowing from it, he added, 'If the doctor asks me a fool's question, I am determined to give a rogue's answer, as if he could dig away in my leg, and try to tear out my bones, and I not feel it.'

They were brave, noble, unselfish fellows. May the virtues which shone so brightly on the battlefield, and still more in the Hospital wards, never be dimmed by drunkenness and crime! Surely men capable of such virtue ought not to sink into drunken sots. Yet how many old pensioners, who have shown heroic courage and more heroic endurance, become in old age useless, degraded drunkards. Can nothing be done to save them from so unworthy a fate, to lead them to spend the rest of their days in a way more worthy of the noble qualities they have been shown to possess? Have they done and suffered so much only to end so poorly? I felt astonished when I considered that these men, so gentle and so generous, so devoid it seemed of coarse rude ways—men who never seemed guilty of an unseemly word or gesture, from whose lips we never heard one word unbecoming gentlemen and Christians—that these noble heroes should not be the chosen of our land, but rather the refuse—not men trained in religion and virtue, but often taken from the lowest and most disorderly of the population, picked up in public-houses, and too often in drunkenness. Comparing these men to others more happily situated, who have been shielded and sheltered, who had been taught much, perhaps spoken much, of their nearness to God and to Christ, who had professed high things, and been mercifully shielded from open sin, the untutored, unprofessing soldiers seemed practically the better Christians, more Christlike, more patient, more humble, more unselfish. It recalled to us the many passages in Holy Scripture, where the publican, the Sadducee, and the Samaritan are preferred to the high professing, boasting Pharisee. No doubt the best and gentlest side of their character was called out in their intercourse with their nurses, but among patients in hospitals at home I have not found such invariable patience and thankfulness. Often among the very lowest I have found heroic and saintly conduct, but here it was the rule, almost, if not quite, without exception.

My half corridor and wards held about sixty patients when quite full, as it was the whole time I was there. It was the half quarter of the lower range, the sixteenth of the whole Hospital, which if every part were equally full (which I believe was the case) must have contained 960 patients.[20] I believe the number at times rose to 1,000. This was too crowded for proper ventilation. The Barrack Hospital seemed to become gradually more crowded than the General, and the air more tainted. They lay close to each other on each side of the corridors, leaving merely room to pass between. I do not know how many this vast building contained. One might walk almost miles along sick and dying men. The whole army seemed becoming victims to the war, or rather to the want of foresight and arrangements for their support and comfort, to fatigue, cold, damp, and hunger.

'Ah!' said one of the poor sufferers, 'the pride of England is laid low; she has sent forth the flower of her children, the

Dr. Smith's ambulance waggons at the siege of Sebastopol

A corridor in the Barrack Hospital
From the *Illustrated London News* 16 December, 1854

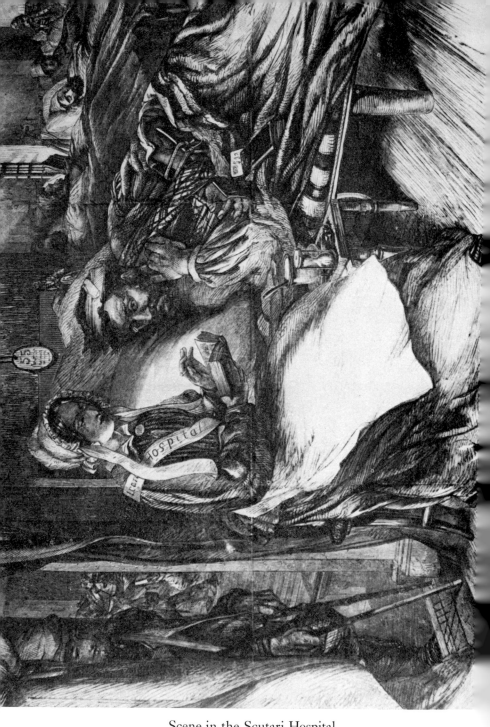

Scene in the Scutari Hospital

young, the brave, and the beautiful, and she will never see them more.'

Looking up at that vast prison-like building, we thought, within these gloomy walls lie the wreck of one of the noblest armies Britain ever sent forth. Here where they landed last spring, full of health and spirits, of gaiety and hope, and danced and sung and kept holiday, full of self-confidence, admired by the natives for their height, fair complexion, unlike our dark, diminutive allies (who did not differ in size or complexion much from the Turks); here within a few months they return—how different, health and strength for ever gone, worn out, wasted, dying, and after a few days or weeks of feeble languishing here they were laid to rest.

But most of my patients in the General Hospital, at least of the wounded, did recover, and I trust are now safe and happy at home. Only one of my wounded died in the Hospital, and I afterwards heard that one died on his passage home. He was a brave little lad, Samuel Gregg, about seventeen, who had lost his right arm and left hand at Inkerman. He was a cheerful, contented boy, and never lost heart, notwithstanding his helpless, handless condition. He was slightly framed, and seemed of delicate constitution; but his two stumps healed rapidly, and he seemed full of youthful buoyancy.

'I'll be all right,' he used to say, 'when I get to my mother.' He dictated a letter to his parents, which appeared in *The Times*, telling of his misfortune, but full of cheerful hope and spirit, telling them not to be anxious, as he was doing wonderfully, and hoped soon to be with them. Of course he was very helpless, and unable to feed himself.

A man in the next bed was equally disabled. He had lost one arm, the other was completely shattered. On another bed near lay a lad with both legs shot through. He told me when they were first examined the doctors said both legs must come off, and were preparing to remove them when an ambulance of more pressing cases came up, and they said his legs must remain as they were for the present; he could have them taken off at Scutari if he lived to get there. He not only did so, but his legs were so much better when he arrived that amputation was considered unnecessary; indeed, though stiff and lame for life, he was one of the first wounded to recover and be sent home. He told me an interesting story of his enlisting to be near an elder brother of whom he was very fond.

Sam Gregg was never down-hearted; his companions in the Hospital were very kind to him, and waited on him and fed him. It was very touching to see the maimed waiting on and helping each other. A man of the 47th, who was severely wounded in the thigh, was particularly kind to Sam, and watched him with a sort of fatherly interest. This man was from the neighbourhood of Bristol, and was about thirty. He was well educated, and told me that he and some others clubbed together and got an Italian master when they were quartered in Malta.

He admired Miss Nightingale, and used to ask me about her. 'Is it not beautiful,' he said, 'to hear her speak Italian?'

Like the others, his heart in sickness seemed to yearn after his mother; his eyes glistened as he spoke of her. 'When it pleases God to take my father, won't I do my duty to her, and make her comfortable?'

Thinking from his account she might be removed first, I said, in that case I hoped he would do his duty and be a comfort to his father.

'Oh yes,' he said, 'but I don't seem to think so much of him. I do hope to be a comfort to my mother.'

One day this poor man wished to give Sam some bread and butter (butter was a great treat, being seldom seen in the wards), but the poor man could not reach it, as it lay on the window-sill, and he could not move, and Sam having no hands, could only stand looking wistfully at it. No one else was near, but seeing the difficulty from a distance, I fetched the bread and butter and put them in the poor lame man's hands, and he proceeded to spread and cut it, and to feed his poor helpless young friend.

Sarah Anne's Journal

The men used to tease Sam in a friendly way, and he always took it pleasantly and with good temper. They advised him to marry, and asked how he would put on his bride's ring.

'I'll manage it some way if necessary,' he said, laughing; 'but I'll be all right when I get home to my mother.'

He never reached that longed-for home and mother. He was shipped off in December, and went in high spirits, promising I should hear of his reaching home. He kept his promise. When dying, he asked a comrade to write and tell me of his death. The brave boy died at sea, and rests in the deep. The cause of his death was not stated. I fear in the crowded ship he would not have the attendance his helpless state required. He was a cheerful, merry-hearted lad, making the best of everything, and ready to enjoy a joke even against himself. He told me that at home in Derbyshire he went regularly to Sunday school and church, but that he had not given much attention to religion since he joined the army. I think he told me that the day he underwent his double operation a Roman Catholic priest spoke kindly to him.

At this time I think we had only one chaplain belonging to the Church of England in the General Hospital. Sam admired the devotion of the Roman Catholic priests, though regarding the value of their ministrations with strong Protestant feeling. They were more numerous than our chaplains, and seemed very zealous in discharge of their duties, grave and polite to us. They used to bow and say 'God bless you!' to us in passing in the passages and wards, which I felt very kind, and unlike the conduct of the Roman ecclesiastics I have met in visiting the poor cholera patients at Plymouth in England, when the Roman Catholic bishop denounced poor dying sufferers for allowing us to nurse them, though he provided no one else to do it.

'Shure, your riverence,' said one dying man, 'I thought they were true Catholics.' After this he called together his flock, and warned them, as they valued their eternal welfare, to avoid and reject our services. One or two rebelled and remonstrated.

'If these good people come to help and serve us when every one else forsakes us, we cannot promise to drive them away.'

'If you prefer a few attentions to your poor perishing bodies to your soul's eternal happiness, receive them, but if not, reject them,' was his last command.

The priests at Scutari acted more kindly and more wisely. Some of the Roman Catholic patients seemed well informed, some very devout and prayerful, some ignorant and careless. One poor dying man showed me a medal the priest had given him.

He said: 'I am what is called a Roman Catholic; I know no better. I would as soon be a Protestant if I knew how; but since I have been ill, I have been more attentive to my duties than I ever was before.'

And playing with his medal, he added, 'It is a very pretty piece of gold.'

The priest entering at that moment, asked me for a string to fasten the medal to the poor man's neck. I produced a bit of red tape. As he put it on, Sam Gregg whispered to me, with a smile, 'I don't think much of that gammon! What good can a medal do to a dying man?'

Towards the end of December some of the wounded recovered so far as to be sent home, and were succeeded by sick and dying men who rapidly made way for others. Sometimes one bed was filled and emptied several times in the course of one week, men being brought in merely to die. One Irish dragoon, called M'Cabe, recovered about this time, and was sent home. He was wounded at Balaclava in the Heavy Cavalry charge, some very severe ones all sword or lance. He told me he thought he was doing such wonders, he remained among the enemy while his companions passed on, till he found himself alone among them and surrounded. Feeling wounds on all sides, he said he offered himself up to God, and using the spur, knocked down two of the crowd round him and escaped, his sword hand almost cut off, a deep cut on the shoulder, a lance thrust in the side, another cut across the face injuring the check bone and almost cutting off the nose, and nine smaller cuts and thrusts. His hand was the worst; it got into a very bad state, and was disabled for life.

This man was an example of quiet patience, letting the doctor do as he pleased as to cutting and probing his wounds, even the one on his face, without shrinking. He said, 'Won't I think of my friends the Russians when I look in a looking-glass as long as I live!'

Sometimes the cries of anguish from the poor men (especially when the doctor was trying to remove balls left in the wound) were very harrowing, but they were generally suppressed, the doctor being impatient of any outcry, and giving chloroform for severe operations. I have seen young fellows flush and shed tears from pain, but without cry or groan. The cries from some parts of the Hospital were heart-rending.

The patients brought in during December were in a very bad state—some dying, some in a state of filth no words can describe, miserable skeletons devoured by lice. One day one such sad object was brought in and laid on the floor in one of my wards while the orderlies came to ask me what should be done. Could he bear a bath? I drew near, and could scarcely believe the thing lying on the ground was a human being, much less a man still young, and as one of his regiment standing by told me, one who very lately was as fine looking a young man as ever stepped. This comrade had received a wound at the Alma, and escaping the subsequent hardship of the camp, was in full health. He looked with tears on his poor comrade, and said:

'This is worse than any battle, these are the most fearful fruits of war.'

Seeing the wretched state of the sick and frostbitten, and hearing of the sad state of the army, the wounded saw it was well they had escaped the hardships and miseries of the camp before Sebastopol. Several of the poor men died within an hour of their arrival, some never spoke. The poor man to whom the orderlies called my attention was quite sensible and could speak in a hollow sepulchral voice. His ragged flannel seemed alive and moving with lice, he was caked in living dirt, his back was raw, and he was wasted to a skeleton. As he was too exhausted to bear a bath we cut off his flannel shirt and had him lifted on his bed, and then I washed his face and hands, which were caked and buried in filth and lice; he seemed scarcely able to bear even this, though he liked it. I then fed him with a little soup, and the chaplain came and prayed with him. He and several of the same shipload died the ensuing night.

These deeply diseased and dying men were brought in and laid beside poor wounded men, some of whom were peculiarly susceptible to depression and infection, and it seemed very undesirable for them to be subjected to such scenes. One young lad of the Rifles, who was severely wounded in the thigh by a shell, and lay in a very depressed and precarious state, had the bed next him filled by a succession of dying men. A new case of fearful disease and death was laid beside him every day, and being nervous and susceptible, this greatly impeded his recovery. A noble fellow who was also in a very delicate state lay on the other side of these dying men, and on my regretting to him and on his account that such cases should be laid beside him, he answered:

'Oh! it is painful to see one's poor comrades in such a state, but I should be a sorry fellow if I were not glad to see them brought in to get a little care and kindness in their last hours.'

It seems strange we could witness such scenes and sufferings calmly, but to us as to the poor sufferers there seemed granted a calm and quiet temper and a sort of stunned feeling, for had we realised all their sad sufferings, all their bright hopes and young lives, all the love and care of wives and mothers all quenched in misery and death, we could not have borne it. We saw there what noble children our country could produce —noble in appearance, in character, and in conduct; and we saw them crushed to death by cruel improvidence and neglect.

One night I found a fine-looking Irishman who had lately

arrived sitting up in bed with oppressed and labouring breath, evidently suffering from inflammation of the chest. As the doctors in their evening rounds did not generally examine minutely each case as in the morning, but only attended to those they were anxious about, passing the others quickly in the dark, I sent to beg his attention to this man, and he came and ordered a blister.[21] The poor man seemed suffering and in distress, and thinking he would die, he asked me to take charge of five sovereigns he had by him, and to take his directions as to their disposal and as to other money. I did so rather unwillingly, feeling my health and life so uncertain, and that they might give way any day, as indeed did occur as regards health, for before his recovery I became so ill of fever that my death was expected, and I was quite deaf and almost insensible. However, he expressed no anxiety and made no inquiry, till on my recovery I remembered his trust and sent it to him.

About this time the only death among my wounded occurred. A much larger proportion both of sick and of wounded died in the adjoining wards, which I attributed chiefly to their having frequent change of doctor, no female nurse, and very young and careless orderlies. As they carried their dead through our corridor I have heard my men say:

'What do you fellows do down there to get rid of your patients so fast? I doubt you don't give them fair play.'

Certainly we had the same doctor almost all the time I was there, and he was careful, skilful, and most attentive to diet.

The young wounded man who died was George Nicol of the Grenadier Guards. He was of a very large frame, yet had a delicately fair complexion. His wound did not seem severe, it was in the heel of his foot, and it healed well and closed up. I think this too rapid healing caused his death, resulting in blood-poisoning or pyemia. About a fortnight before his death, when apparently doing well, he told me he was dying, and begged me to take charge of his watch and money to send home to his little brother Benjamin. I told him I thought he would recover, but on his earnest entreaties I took the watch (which was a Russian one), and gave it to Miss Nightingale's care. At this time he had fits of ague [malaria], but otherwise he seemed pretty well. His appetite, however, was poor, and he took little but the arrowroot I made for him with egg and milk, which he liked, and used to watch for, saying to me, 'I watch and long for you as a cat for a mouse.' A day before his death I saw him put his money in a little bag and fasten it round his neck. On the same day and about the same hour a colour-sergeant of the Scots Greys died. After George Nicol's death I asked the orderly about his money, but as I could not hear of it, and he had begged me to see it was sent to his brother, meeting the chaplain I mentioned the circumstances to him, and on his insisting the orderly produced it, but in many cases I fear the dead and dying were robbed.

Great numbers now came in dying; some rallied for a little, and then sunk suddenly, their feet turning black some time before death;[22] others never rallied, but sunk at once. Several were very fine looking young men of the Guards and Cavalry, others quite young lads frost-bitten and diarrhœa cases, some so worn-out, miserable, and filthy as to have lost all traces of manhood, even of humanity. When we first came most of the patients in the Barrack Hospital still wore their military regimental cap, and their pale, ghastly, wasted faces under the warlike head-dress had a strange weird effect. When death was evidently approaching, they so often said they felt so easy and so much better, that such feelings and expressions seemed to us to forebode the nearness of the end.

One little lad lingered long. The doctor said to me one day: 'I can do nothing for him—medicine seems of no use; do you give him frequently a little beef-tea.'

I did so, feeding him every few hours.

The next day the doctor said he was better, and desired me to continue. I did so with good effect, though he occasionally relapsed, and I heard that soon after I was taken ill he died. His name was Joe Martin. Though not an engaging lad in look or manner, he was, I trust, a good one. One night I found him weeping bitterly, and trying to comfort him, he sobbed out:

'I'm going to die, and my father and mother did love me so.'

Another evening I spoke to him, and receiving no answer, repeated my question, when I saw he was engaged with a prayer-book; he only raised his eyes, gave me a glance of reproof, and continued reading. In a few seconds, having finished, he quietly shut his book and answered. He was very fond of sewing, patching, &c., and used to show me his performances with childlike pleasure.

Some of the patients were very ignorant, especially some Irish and English; others, on the contrary, were well informed, and in education and general information seemed much above the average of civilians in their rank. Many were in language and manner gentlemen, and none were boorish except a few evidently raw recruits. The orderly the doctor assigned to me was of this class—an English ploughboy, with heavy horny hands from which the wounded used to shrink. He used to fetch and empty my water, and was fonder of pawing wounded limbs than their owners approved.

'Keep your hands off; they are like a pound of lead,' they would say.

He was, however, good-natured, patient, and attentive.

There was great variety of character among the patients— the heavy clumsy English ploughboy, the sharp street-bred London boy, the canny cautious Scot, the irresistibly amusing Irishman with his brogue and bulls. Certainly estimable as they are, the Scotch were in general the least attractive patients —silent, grave, cold, and cautious, they were not so winning as the Irish, with their quick feeling and ready wit.

'But ne'er in battlefield throbs heart more brave
Than that which beats beneath the Scottish plaid.'

So says their great fellow-countryman, and many a battlefield proves the truth of his words. In the Hospital it was impossible to say which excelled in virtue. All behaved nobly.

One might be pleasanter and more amusing than another, one more or less sensitive than another, but all were brave, patient, noble, grateful, and generous. There was no strict type of national character. We had rough ignorant Scots, others well educated and well read; English boors and English gentlemen; Irish lads scarcely able to express themselves in English, and Irish veterans who spoke with fluency and eloquence. There were in my part several men of the Scots Greys, and also of the 42nd [Black Watch] and 93rd [Highlanders], fine noble men, who had fought bravely and suffered patiently. The wife of one of the 42nd had followed her husband. She seemed a very respectable woman, but the position of the poor wives was most uncomfortable—good and bad seemed huddled together, and some were very bad, so that I heard many were ordered home, and some into confinement till they could be shipped off. Those who were clever and industrious as well as respectable could earn a good deal, unless (as was generally the case) they had a young and sickly baby to attend to.

One afternoon early in December the Duke of Cambridge[23] visited both Hospitals. As he passed, along with a number of officers, Murphy made bold to address him, 'I thank God I see your Royal Highness so well.' The Duke inquired into his regiment, his wounds, &c., ending, according to Murphy, by saying he was 'a fine-looking fellow'.

A little further on the Duke noticed Aslett, and a fresh patient next him, who had been brought in that day, and whom the Turks with cruel carelessness had thrown out of his stretcher on the stone pier, and so very much smashed and disfigured his face. He was a sad object. Dirt, exposure, and disease had wasted and disfigured his face and form, and this finishing stroke of his bearers smashed it; but like the others no sense of injury seemed to possess his heart—grateful for every kind word or act, however unavailing, not even this rough unfeeling treatment seemed to have power to irritate him. The Duke, however, was indignant. He asked how the poor fellow came by that face, and hearing how it was, he relieved his feelings by committing the Turks to perdition. This poor man died a few days after. He had a complication of diseases, dysentery and scurvy, and the remedies for scurvy seemed to aggravate his other disorder and accelerate death.

On first arriving he was ravenously hungry and anxious for food, saying he had little or nothing on board ship. They had no regular diet till the third day after their arrival, though we were often allowed to supply those who wanted it with broth or arrowroot soon after they were got to bed. But on this poor man expressing hunger, and nothing being ready, Aslett in the next bed offered him all that was left of his bread, knowing no more could be had till next day. He devoured it ravenously, dry and sour as it was, and looked round for more. Presently I got him a little arrowroot. Aslett took a tender interest in him, as he did in all his fellow-sufferers, especially those who were most weak and suffering.

Next morning, about the time for arrowroot, Aslett said to me, 'Perhaps my arrowroot will do him good,' and began to ask anxiously if it were coming. The orderly got cross, and grumbled at his persistent inquiries.

'Can't you be quiet, ye glutton; do you think a fellow has nothing to do but fetch and carry for you?'

Aslett made no answer, but seeing his flushed anxious face and tearful eye, I said to the orderly:

'Don't speak so sharply; Aslett does not want the arrowroot for himself, but for the poor man next him.'

As soon as the arrowroot came, Aslett gave it to me, and also some of his wine, and I mixed them, and fed his poor friend, he looking on with benevolent satisfaction. From his good appetite I had some hopes of this poor man's recovery, but about the fourth day he began to sink. I used to feed him; indeed, unless I did so, those weak as he was were little benefited by their food. The orderly threw down the food, or laid it carelessly perhaps out of reach and out of sight of the patient, and if he was too weak or too languid to feed himself, there it lay till the orderly came again to remove it. They would not think it necessary to feed any, except the few who had both arms disabled, and some of the other nurses told me that in their wards, even when the orderlies were kind and wished to feed those too ill to feed themselves, they did not know how to proceed; they crammed them instead of giving a little at a time, and they had no idea of making the food palatable by little changes.

This poor man's last words to me were, 'God Almighty bless, and reward you for all you have done for me.' I had done so little for him, poor dear fellow, and had so often pained him in putting food into his cut and bruised lips and mouth, that I said involuntarily, 'Oh no,' and then was sorry, as he seemed vexed and perplexed.

Aslett was ever alive to the wants and sufferings of his companions, and anxious for their relief, and so unostentatious in his kindness and generosity, I think no one knew of it but me. He was also modest and delicate as to his own wants and sufferings. He told me the wounds and bedsores I dressed healed faster than those the orderly did for him, but when on hearing this I offered to do them all for him, he coloured and said, 'No, thank you, I had rather not, thank you all the same,' so that I could not press it.

One afternoon the chaplain came into my ward and asked me to go to a distant part of the Hospital to attend to a patient who was in great need of a nurse. I hesitated a moment, as my part had been assigned to me, and I was not at liberty to go to any other part of the Hospital, as Miss Nightingale had given each division in charge to a particular nurse, except one part, the doctor of which disliked and objected to female nurses. So I mentioned this to the chaplain, who seemed vexed at any demur, though I said if the patient were in the part assigned to no nurse, and was in extreme distress, I was willing to incur the risk of blame and go. He asked who had command of the nurses in this Hospital. I said, I know of no one in command but Miss Nightingale. He gave me the poor man's name and direction, and I promised it should be attended to. I then went into the next ward and mentioned the circumstance to the lady in charge, who happened to be Sister Jean de Chantel.

On telling her I had said no one was in command but Miss Nightingale, she immediately said:

'Sister Mary de Gonzaga has the command in this Hospital.'

I answered, 'I was not aware of that; I was never told so. At all events she is not here to-day.'

So we agreed to go together, and that if the poor patient were a Roman Catholic she should attend to his wants; if not, I should. He proved not a Roman Catholic, and I did what I could for him.

About this time I was called to read and pray with a dying man anxious to be prayed with. After doing so, the poor fellow thanked me, and pressed on me some of his wine as a reward, saying, 'It is very good, and I am sure you have made a beautiful prayer.'

Of course no difference as to the patient's faith was made with regard to dressing wounds, &c., and I am not aware of the patients having any scruple or choice as to their nurse's faith. Some (of the Scotch especially) might feel a little antipathy to the dress of the nuns, associated as it was in their minds with Romanism, and some of the Irish might perhaps prefer them, but in general I know the gentle cheerful manner of the nuns overcame all such antipathy, while I and the other Anglicans found their favourite and most affectionately grateful patients among the Irish and Roman Catholics. But I had a feeling of national and ecclesiastical independence that I would rather not be under command of a Roman Catholic nun, and on relating this circumstance to Miss Nightingale, I expressed the feeling that however I might personally respect and admire the nuns, I had reasons for wishing not to be under their command or direction. Miss N. explained that I was not to consider myself in any way under the command of Sister M. de G., but was to consult her, *i.e.*, Miss N., alone in any difficulty, and that the charge given to Sister M. related only to the outward conduct of the nurses, and not to us. Sister M. was inclined to take rather more authority than this, though on the whole she exercised it with gentleness and wisdom, and was very considerate and yielding.

The fresh walk between the Hospitals I felt very conducive to health, and for the first two months at Scutari I felt more than usually well; the air seemed bracing, and though the food was far from tempting, I always felt ready for it, and able to manage it. We used to set out about 8.30 A.M., and return at 1 P.M. In the afternoon we went at two and returned at five, when we had tea, after which I accompanied Sister Elizabeth, who was again employed in the Barrack Hospital under Mr Maclean. Miss Langston, Harriet Erskine, and Clara continued in the Barrack Hospital, where the sick were accumulating in great numbers; indeed, but for the rapid transfer from the Hospital to the Cemetery, there would have been no room even in that vast pile of building for the shiploads of sick coming daily across the Black Sea. That sea itself became the grave of thousands. Sometimes on account of the Hospitals being full, and of the difficulties in landing, these sad cargoes lay on board ship for days after reaching Scutari; of course numbers being daily thrown overboard, and thus lessening the difficulty in accommodating those who survived. Seeing the state of filth and neglect these poor men were in when landed, hearing how often they had implored in vain for a cup of water, of the relief and comfort the presence of some soldiers' wives had given in one ship, and these men saying they owed their lives to their ministrations, made me long for some organised plan for supplying the transports with female nurses, but at that time it was impossible. I hope our country may yet procure women capable of such trust and training. Why, when our countrywomen as individuals equal those of any nation, should they be incapable of forming a society such as the French Sisters of Charity or the German Deaconesses?[24]

Sister Bertha, Margaret, and I continued to be employed in the General Hospital. As the wounded went home they were succeeded by sick, and on this account, and also because a body of young men called dressers[25] appeared on the stage, we had fewer wounds to dress, but we found no want of employment. During the afternoon the work was lighter, feeding some of the weaker ones, reading to or oftener writing for others, and doing many other little nameless offices as required. It was the orderly's duty to do all the heaviest part of nursing —lifting the men, making the beds (which was not often performed), bringing up the food, carrying away and washing up —also washing and cleaning those disabled or too weak to do it themselves; but this was much neglected, and I used to do it rather than insist on the rough unwilling services of the orderly. In the evening Sister Elizabeth allowed me to help her in carrying night drinks to her sick, and to accompany her on her rounds.

At this time she was not quite happy from thinking Miss Nightingale was not satisfied with her, which was, I fear, in a measure true. Sister E. was ardent, impulsive, excitable, and over-anxious, and though Miss Nightingale appreciated some of her good qualities, she did not know her previously so as to value her fully, and her impatience, enthusiasm, and want of caution made her troublesome.

Talleyrand's words, 'surtout point de zèle', seemed a ruling maxim in high quarters, and the nuns, sisters, and nurses being suspected of this capital crime I believe Miss N. had difficulty in holding out and preventing the whole body being condemned and dismissed *en masse* for indiscretion and 'trop de zèle'. Some one at least must be sacrificed, 'pour encourager les autres', and Sister Elizabeth was the chosen victim— generous, brave, noble, unselfish Sister Elizabeth.

When we first came and found the men so suffering and in want of common necessaries, she wrote to a relative detailing the wants and sufferings of the patients, and begging for comforts for them. This letter her relative sent to *The Times*, and it seemed a prelude or keynote to the chorus of complaint that soon rang through England and roused popular indignation against Government and the conductors of the war against all in authority—for evils which it were scarcely in their power to foresee or prevent. The heads of management or of mismanagement at Scutari, seeing this letter, inquired as to the writer, and required that she should be subjected to examination. So poor Sister E., with her honest, generous, trusting heart and incautious tongue, was placed before three doctors and a lawyer to be examined as to the truth of her letter.[26] She had no copy of her letter, was never told what misstatements she was accused of, and was wholly unprepared for this trial.[27] Few people, I think, writing in the midst of exciting and heart-rending scenes, would be able, after seven or eight weeks passed in active work, in the midst of interesting and exciting scenes, to remember distinctly and relate without discrepancy minute facts and events. To do so, would prove almost miraculous powers of memory; not to do so, prove nothing but the existence of human infirmity. But these gentlemen decided otherwise, they pronounced her letter incorrect and contradictory to her verbal evidence, and therefore that she was an untruthful, prevaricating person, who ought to be dismissed.

I felt this a most unjust and ungentlemanly proceeding, still more so when the very next day she was ordered on board ship to return to England. On the evening of the 23rd December she was condemned; that very evening I accompanied her round her wards for the last time, and on the 24th, Christmas Eve, she was sent on board ship. It was a sudden and overwhelming sorrow to our party, and to me especially. Clara was also ordered home and obeyed with the utmost good-humoured alacrity. I suppose it was the state of her hands caused her dismissal, they certainly disqualified her in great measure for nursing.

Sister Elizabeth's removal we all felt as at once a grief and an insult. Loving and admiring Sister E. at all times, I loved and admired her far more for the Christian temper she showed under reproach and wrong. *We* were indignant, but she refused to join in blaming any one; she only regretted leaving her

Florence Nightingale receiving the wounded at Scutari
From a painting by Jerry Barratt

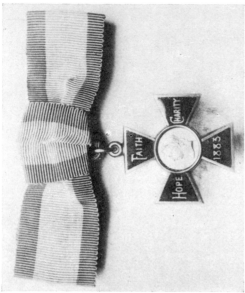

The Royal Red Cross received by Sarah Anne

Sarah Anne with Alice Terrot at Balmoral after their presentation to Queen Victoria

patients, and having caused trouble and annoyance to Miss Nightingale. But her generous unselfish conduct increased my indignation and grief that one so valuable and so noble should be accused of and condemned for that of which she was utterly incapable. To be deprived of her whose society I felt as my greatest happiness and comfort, whose presence I had hoped for as my greatest earthly comfort if God pleased to send me sickness and death in that distant land, to lose her anyhow I felt a sore trial, but that she, the noblest and best, should go in disgrace, was almost more than I could bear. They wished also to make her confess herself guilty of untruth, threatening her with penal consequences if not doing so; but in this she was firm, utterly refusing to sign some confession laid before her, saying she could not truthfully say she was conscious of untruth, whatever might be the consequences of her refusing to do so.

I asked leave to see her embark, and on reaching the little pier we found the five white Norwood nuns and two nurses who were being sent home for different reasons. It was a dark, wet, stormy evening as we stood on the little rough pier waiting for the boat, wet and cold and sad. At last it came, and they embarked on the stormy sea, and I turned towards our quarters, alone, sick at heart and desolate, and from that time I never felt quite well.

It was a sad Christmas to us all. We received Holy Communion, and in the evening I went down to Sister E.'s wards to do a few commissions for her, and wrote for one of her men, a fine-spirited lad who after detailing in his letter the hardships he had endured, and the wounds he had received, ended by saying the only things he wanted now were a little tobacco, and that his wounds would heal quickly and let him back to his duty before Sebastopol, before it fell. I could not tell the men Sister Elizabeth was gone, so I left them in ignorance, but I told Mr Maclean, who seemed indignant. He was suffering himself from injustice on the part of his superiors, and we agreed this should teach us to look above earthly superiors. I saw no more of this excellent devoted young man. He asked me to express to Sister Elizabeth his grateful sense of the value of her services, and his regret for their loss, and said he wished to write himself.

I think he was from Edinburgh,[28] and had been a pupil of Dr Richard Mackenzie, of whom he spoke with enthusiastic affection and admiration. I asked if he knew him.

'Knew him!' he said, 'I think I did; his death is the greatest loss we have had, the greatest misfortune. A warm bath might have saved him, Mackenzie said so himself. When we were encamped in Bulgaria, Mackenzie came into my tent one night and said to me, "Maclean, if I live to return I will strive to have some change in the management of medical affairs in the army."'

It had long been proposed to send a party to reside in the General Hospital, but I believe there was a difficulty as to which lady was to be placed at the head. Miss Nightingale at one time fixed on Sister Elizabeth, but Sister E. mentioned the plan to Dr M. [Menzies], who expressed his regret that she should leave the Barracks, on which she said it was not her wish to go, as she would regret leaving her patients. On which Dr M. repeated to Miss N. his wish that she should remain at the Barracks, alleging that Sister E. did not wish to go. Miss N. asked me if I were willing to go to live at the General Hospital if our party were divided, some remaining where they were. I said I was willing to go where she thought it desirable.

A short time after this, two nuns, a nurse, and I were detained at the General Hospital till it grew dark, and we found our charioteer, tired of waiting, had gone home and left us. It was a snowy, stormy night, and the elder nun, dreading to go home in the dark, applied to Dr O'. [O'Flaherty], the chief doctor at the General Hospital, who begged us to remain, and said he would do all in his power to make us comfortable, and send a messenger to the Barracks to account for our non-appearance, and prevent any anxiety as to our fate. Then we set to work to make ourselves comfortable by lighting a charcoal brazier, which produced more smoke than heat, but we sat round it till we vanished from each other in a thick mist. In time, however, it dispersed, the fire burnt, and we set ourselves to make tea at a little round table with tea equipage and food the doctor kindly sent us. He then came to see if we were comfortable, and to see how many stretchers he should send, which rather amused the younger nun, as that term was generally applied to the litter for removing the dead.

'We hope to need no stretchers just yet,' she said, 'but will be thankful for bedding for four.'

The poor nurse who was with us came with Miss Stanley. Her husband was a soldier in the Grenadier Guards, and was brought a patient into the Hospital about the same time his wife arrived, so she was just in time to nurse him at the last, for he died in a few days. This poor man, though ignorant of his wife's arrival or even that she intended coming, said to one of the nurses on the day of his arrival:

'There's my wife walking in the garden, go and tell her to come to me.'

She thought his mind was wandering, but his wife did come to him that very day.

The nuns made their bed in the big room, I made mine in an adjoining closet, and the nurse spent most of the night by her husband's bedside. The nuns were at all times cheerful, pleasant companions, and I had a pleasant evening. After retiring to my closet I heard the nuns say Compline together, and knowing the office, I joined them in heart, especially in those beautiful words, 'Into Thy hands, O God, we commend our spirits, for Thou hast redeemed us O Lord Thou God of Truth.' Afterwards I thought of our charcoal brazier still burning and of the danger of suffocation and begged Sister Mary would extinguish it. She seemed amused at my anxiety, and assured me she was innocent of charcoal plots.

Next morning we rose, had breakfast, and went to our wards as usual, our friends from the Barracks comfortably assuring us they had never missed or been in the least anxious about us. A few days after this one evening as we were returning to the Barracks we met Mrs C., who gave us a message from Miss Nightingale desiring us to return and remain at the General Hospital to live and sleep there, so we returned and made up our beds. I was thankful for this change to be under the same roof with my patients and to be able to spend the evening among them; also because the Barracks were to me painfully full of the remembrance of Sister Elizabeth. I never passed along the corridor without recalling her stately form with whom I had so often passed through them, nor without regretting her absence and her fate.

In the General Hospital we had two large rooms given us, one to the sisters and ladies, one to the nurses, and a smaller one to the nuns. Our room was one on the left hand on the entrance of the Hospital. It was lofty, but being on the ground floor, and the General Hospital itself lying a good deal lower than the Barracks, our room was, I think, less healthy than our old quarters in the Barrack Tower. The day after we arrived, Miss A. [Anderson] (sister of Sir Charles A.), who came with Miss Stanley's party, came as head of the nurses at the General Hospital, and Sister Mary was transferred to the Barracks. Five nuns who had come with Miss Stanley came to the General Hospital. I believe they were of the same order, but not from the same house as our former friends, and though equally courteous, they were less frank and amusing, and so at least while I was there not such general favourites. Some other nuns of Miss Stanley's party came to the General Hospital on a visit; they seemed remarkably pleasing and winning in manner. Miss Stanley and others of her party became Roman Catholics on their return to England. I do not know how far the conduct of the nuns—and their influence effected this.

A new Hospital was opened at Kulilee,[29] which gave employment to these nuns and others of Miss Stanley's party. There was some mistake as to this party. They arrived before arrangements had been made as to their reception and employment; and, on arriving, instead of having the work they longed for, they were told they were 'not wanted,' and sent to live at Terapia in idleness, a most painful and trying position. The chaplain there was not friendly. He preached at them, describing them, to their great amusement and amazement as 'wolves in sheep's clothing, snakes in glittering skins'. One lady, Miss A., a loyal Church-woman, asked his sanction for visiting the patients. He said she might, but he thought 'she would do more harm than good'.

Another lady, Miss T.,[30] a Unitarian in creed, lent a copy of Keble's *Christian Year* to a young sick officer, a cousin of hers. The chaplain, seeing it on the table, took it up, and asked to take it with him, and on promise of soon returning it gained permission. But afterwards being asked for it, he said he could not return it, as he wished to send it to the War Office to show what popery was being disseminated! This lady was in my illness most kind to me, and Margaret frequently said in reference to her, 'The unbeliever is the best Christian in the room.' I heard that some busybody wrote to the War Office complaining of this lady's religious opinions, but was told the nurses were free to hold any opinions as long as they let others hold their own, and did their duty as nurses.[31]

At Terapia some of the ladies and nurses gained a little relief from *ennui* by going to wash at the Sailor Hospital. They had asked for employment, and this was offered. The nurses were inclined to reject the offer. It was not the work they wanted; but on Miss S. S.[32] saying she would go for one, nine nurses volunteered, so a party of ten went daily. I heard that Miss S. S. took the dirtiest and hardest things to encourage her companions, but being unaccustomed to such work, she wet herself more than necessary.

After this, this party gradually found employment, some in private nursing, some in the Hospital at Kulilee. Besides which, Lord Raglan had applied for nurses at Balaclava,[33] and some of Miss Stanley's party volunteered to go. Miss Nightingale fixed on Miss Langston to head this party, Miss S. S. and

Miss C. [Clough] with her, and five nurses. Miss T., another of Miss Stanley's party, soon after joined us in the General Hospital.

I was now feeling ill, and struggling to shake it off and keep going, and I was thankful to see my men daily recovering. I had every day to pass through half a corridor where there was no female nurse. In passing I often used to speak to some of the poor men, but could do nothing for them. Their doctor was ill, so there was frequent change in their medical attendant, from which they suffered; the orderlies also seemed very young and thoughtless.

On first passing through this corridor, I made acquaintance with some of these men, and it made me sad to see them so neglected. The two first were of the 17th Lancers; they had young, innocent-looking faces. The first was a handsome youth, very severely wounded both in arm and thigh at that disastrous Balaclava charge of the Light Cavalry. A large ball was extracted from his thigh, after it had lain there nearly three months, and though for some time it seemed doing well, his appetite failed, diarrhœa came on, and he died in February after four months' severe suffering.

There was another I was much interested in, a dark, sad-looking youth of the 11th Hussars, who had lost his left leg in the same charge; he looked pale and delicate, and was rather sad and depressed in manner. On asking of his home, he mentioned Berwick; but as he seemed reserved, I desisted questioning him, and only said if he felt too ill to write home, I would be glad to do it for him. He declined with thanks, but said he would be glad of some paper in order to write himself. I got him some, and saw him afterwards sit up, and write a long letter with some difficulty, which I took to Miss Nightingale to be franked. He sank gradually after this, suffering much, his poor stump getting into an awful state. He died early in February. After coming home, I met his mother and sister, and learnt his history. His father was a Berwickshire farmer, who died before his children were settled in life or provided for. Charles, then, a lad pretty well educated, went to London to seek employment; failing to find it, he wrote home saying rather than hang about idle, or return to be a burden on his mother, he would enlist as a private. His mother did not forbid this, and he enlisted in the 11th Hussars, who sometime after were sent to the war. He was well educated, affectionate, and well conducted. His letters home were very interesting, well written, well expressed, and full of kind warm feeling to his home and family. The letter for which I gave him paper contained the most spirited and graphic account I ever read of that glorious but fatal charge which cost him and so many other noble men their limbs and lives.

Another of the 11th Hussars, Robert Martin, who lost his right arm in the same charge, lay in the next bed to Purvis, and they were great friends. I did not know him well in the hospital, but got acquainted with him afterwards. His account of the charge is vivid:

'We were sitting on our horses when Capt. Nolan came galloping up with the order for the Light Brigade to advance and retake the guns that had been captured from the Turks by the Russians. We obeyed, the fire of the enemy from the flank batteries on our right and left became most murderous, while the guns in front were belching forth deadly missiles and making complete streets through our ranks. Ward in front of me was blown to pieces. Turner on my left had his right arm blown off, and afterwards died, and Young on my right also had his right arm blown off. Just then my right arm was shattered to pieces. I gathered it together as well as I could, and laid it across my knees. Glanister unfortunately broke his sword off at the hilt by striking a Russian on the top of his helmet. The order to retire was then given by Sir George Paget, and on turning I perceived a Cossack close to us. He immediately levelled his pistol and fired at Glanister and myself. The ball whizzed past my face and struck Glanister, shattering his underjaw and causing him to fall forward on his cloak, which was rolled up in front of him. The Cossack

bolted at once, and I had presence of mind to grasp the reins of
my horse and put them in my mouth, at the same time seizing
those of Glanister's horse and turning it into the ranks. By
this means no doubt his life was saved. It was now every man
for himself. I galloped back with the remnant of my regiment
and passed through the Polish Lancers who had formed across
our line of retreat. I was beginning to feel faint from loss of
blood, and urged my horse to its utmost speed to get out of
the range of fire; but a spent ball struck my ammunition
pouch, and the next thing I remember was being held up by
an officer and his administering some rum to me which had
the effect of bringing me round. I was then helped off my
horse, put in a stretcher, and carried to the rear. My arm was
afterwards amputated and I was sent to Scutari Hospital, and
carried in there on the 5th November more dead than alive,
my arm having got into a very bad state. Miss Nightingale
came and gave me something which seemed to revive me, and
she afterwards wrote to my friends for me. I recovered and
was sent home to Chatham where I had an attack of Crimean
fever,[34] and on recovering from this I was appointed a
warder in Hampton Court Palace, and married.'[35]

What a lavish waste of life was there! What accumulated
wrecks of hopes and joys, all sacrificed, and for what? Such
thoughts would come as we looked out daily, and saw a long
procession moving to the burying-ground, not of real or of
hired mourners, but merely of the dead and of their bearers,
each corpse carelessly carried, the feet or head often uncovered. Those remains so precious to some heart were borne
along so indifferently, the bearers accustomed to their task
showed no real or affected solemnity of manner, and when
tired they laid their burden down on the ground while they
laughed and chatted. As we watched this daily, and counted a
daily increasing number of lifeless forms, we thought of the
bereaved at home, the mother, wife, and orphan who were yet
to learn their loss. On our first arrival eight was the daily
average of deaths, but they rapidly increased, and soon after

as many died in the comparatively small division we visited; and one day, going by mistake into one of the dead houses (which was next one of our wards), I counted sixteen bodies waiting for interment. It was found impossible to supply soldiers for the duty of bearing the dead to their graves, so Turks were employed. Their rude, noisy way of performing this duty was painful. At last carts were used.

The Rev. S. G. O.[36] was at Scutari for several weeks after our arrival, and indefatigable in ministering spiritually and temporally to the wants of the sufferers. Mr Stafford[37] also was daily in the wards, and seemed very devoted in serving the sick. The poor men in the ward through which I passed seemed left entirely to orderlies, who were mere boys, with all the rough, wild, reckless spirits of boyhood, romping and tearing about as soon as the doctors were out of sight, even in the presence of the dead and dying. More than once I saw poor men sadly neglected here; but I could do nothing but urge the orderlies to be more gentle and attentive. One day as I passed a dying man called to me for a drink; I went to get one, but when I brought it he was dead.

Another lad asked me for a drink, and then to read to him. I did so, and then at his request wrote for him to his friends in Oxford. He asked me to kiss him before he died, and I am sorry I did not. He said one morning:

'It has pleased the Lord to take my comrade in the night, but I am spared a little longer;' but in passing in the evening I spoke to him, and getting no answer, I found he was gone. The men next him did not know it.

When we came Miss Nightingale or Mrs Bracebridge read morning prayers with us and the nurses. The nuns went every morning to Mass. In the evening one of the chaplains read prayers in the large hall with all who were able to attend. Few of the doctors attended on Sunday, but there was a good congregation of wounded officers, &c. There was Holy Communion every Sunday. One doctor—not, I think, a military doctor—went regularly.

The Turks were invariably polite to us, saluting us always with 'Bono Johnnie,' and the women trying to converse; even the little children bringing offerings of fruit and flowers—sweet-mannered, bright-eyed little creatures. One poor man brought us his son, a poor lad covered with sores, and entreated us with the most eloquent and significant gestures to cure him. We could only intercede with the doctors for him, which Sister Mary did, and gained attention and advice. I do not know the result, but the poor man expressed gratitude as touchingly as he had entreated. The children, especially the girls, were generally sweet-looking, graceful little things, who deserved, we felt, a nobler destiny than theirs. But the Turkish women we saw seemed no mere drudges; indeed, as far as we saw, they seemed to live at ease, the men and negroes doing all the hard work. Of course we did not visit the slums, or see anything of the domestic arrangements of the poor; we saw them rather in holiday guise, never toiling, nor in dirt and rags, as too many of our poor women are. I fear the picture many of our soldiers' wives presented of dirt and neglect, of bold rude manners, and of drunkenness, was not calculated to recommend Christianity to the Turks. The poor dogs even seemed friendly to us, and used to follow us whenever we appeared. They did not seem different from English mongrel dogs, and some seemed to have good physical and moral qualities. They seemed very capable of attachment, and to have great confidence in the kind feeling and friendliness of Englishwomen. One especially, a great shaggy fellow, with a broken and badly-mended very crooked leg, formed an especial alliance with us, meeting us every day and accompanying us back and forward from one hospital to the other. His great size made his caresses more flattering than agreeable.

I was sorry when we lost Miss Anderson. Her successor, Miss Smythe, did not remain many weeks. Miss Stanley still wanted more ladies for Kulilee, and some who had come out with her wished to rejoin her. I asked to see Miss Nightingale, to report an occurrence in the General Hospital which seemed to infringe on the rule given as to avoiding proselytism. Margaret had been removed from the ward she had at first, and a nun had succeeded her. One night she asked me to go with her when she visited some of her old friends in the wards she had left, and I consented. As she spoke to a patient I stood at the foot of a bed on which lay a corpse. An orderly came up and said to me:

'That young fellow came in a Protestant, but he died a true Catholic.'

I made no answer, but on Margaret rejoining me, I repeated what the soldier had said. She asked his name, and said she remembered him well, and inquired but could learn no further particulars, except that he had been rebaptized and died a Roman Catholic. Next morning I went with her again, when she visited her old friends, and a poor dying man, lying in the next bed to the one which had been occupied by the lad who died there the previous evening, said to Margaret:

'I wish to say nothing but what is true and kind of any one, nothing that I will regret where I am going, but it did hurt me to see the nuns get round that poor young fellow, and persuade him to join their Church. Poor lad, in his weak state, it was no wonder he should yield. May God forgive them all.'

This was inquired into. It seemed the young man had always been a serious character, and a communicant in the Church of England. The nuns denied having used persuasion; said his change was of God's free grace, and nothing could be proved, though the patients stated that the nuns had shown constant and peculiar attention to this young man.

I began to struggle against nausea, nervous irritability, and feverish headache, but was thankful to see my men rapidly recovering. Donaldson went home; Aslett was sitting up and spoke of getting up, though his poor limbs were still too wasted for that; he was fast gaining flesh and colour. I was deeply thankful for this, for I had never become reconciled to the thought of his death, and prayed earnestly he might recover. And when Murphy said to me one day, 'That poor fellow has suffered long, but it won't be for long now—he is going fast,' though it seemed true, I could not bear to acquiesce, and felt as if he must not die. I gave him cod-liver oil in lemon juice, which seemed to benefit him. The little bugle boy was also thriving on the same regimen; his gentle comrade was sinking. Morton was still in a precarious state. Burnes' leg was better, but he began to suffer from aguish fever. A most venerable looking hero, who had fought in thirteen engagements in India and the Crimea, and who gloried in his profession, Sergeant Schomberg by name, was recovering. My wounded were mostly gone home. The little curly-headed bugle boy was a brave little Scot. His name, I think, was Grant. I thought he was dying of consumption, he was so wasted and had such a cough, but cod-liver oil seemed to restore him. The brave little fellow, when he thought himself dying, longed to be near his mother, but as he regained strength he gave up all thought of going home, and only craved to return to his comrades in the Crimea. The sweet-looking boy who lay opposite to him was a gentle, grateful lad. I wrote for him to his mother. He said to her:

'After all I suffered in the camp and on the voyage, when I got here and was laid on a quiet bed, and the ladies and nurses spoke so kind and tender, I just felt as if I had got to heaven at last.'

Dear gentle lad, I trust he passed to his real and everlasting rest, and that Scutari Hospital, with all its roughness and miseries, was to him the gate of Paradise. I remember his bright sweet look, fair flowing hair, almost heavenly smile, and low gentle voice. The first day I was prevented going to my wards by illness I heard he had died. Aslett's recovery filled me with thankfulness. He told me every day he felt stronger, his eyes glistening with joy and gratitude as he spoke; he began to sleep well at night, which for months he could not do, and his face began to fill up. He still suffered much in his limbs, which seemed mere bones, rough, hard, and stiff as the trunk of a tree; he could not move them, and by lying in one posture they produced much pain. I used to rub them with cod-liver oil, which seemed to relieve him.

The men in this Hospital used to have a clean shirt (or one professing to be such) brought to them every week, but often the one brought as clean had only one sleeve or none, besides they were so washed that the folds and seams were still full of lice and nits. They were washed by the Turks. The doctor asked if I could rectify this, but I could only tell Miss Nightingale. It was very often extremely difficult to get shirts for the newly arrived, who were always miserably filthy. The doctor had to sign a requisition to the wardmaster, which he did, but whether there really was a want of shirts, or that the wardmaster could not find them, the requisitions were often unsuccessful. One day, when five new patients were lying shirtless, the corporal returned with the doctor's requisition dishonoured, saying there were none in store.

'A lie!' said the doctor; 'I saw thousands and thousands in store yesterday. None in store! indeed, that's a convenient answer for people who are too lazy to do their duty.'

He tore the requisition into bits, saying, 'There's the last requisition I shall sign; I shall do my duty as a medical officer in attending to my patients, but never sign another requisition.'

I offered to apply to Miss Nightingale if he would sanction it, but he refused, saying:

'It is the duty of Government to supply these men with shirts; it is not my duty to trouble Miss Nightingale.'

He never would sign a requisition, and I could get no clothing without one, so that I could not help my poor men as to clothing. I saw one of the nuns come and give one of my men come clothes, and I was glad any of them should get help any how. The nuns had freer access to shirts, &c., than I had, from the Rev. Mother having charge of a store. Sister M. de G. several times offered me novels for my men, saying they might interest my men, though the chaplains did not care for their having them, but she thought they were better for them than most pious publications.

About this time one day the doctor, having been touching a wound, called for some water and a towel for his hands. I gave him some water and a basin, but the orderly told him he must sign a requisition for a towel. However, I provided a clean rag, which served his purpose. The distress for shirts soon after our arrival was very great, whole wards seeming shirtless—at least to have that article was a distinction. During this shirt distress an order was given that no one should be buried in a shirt; they were to be taken off before the body was removed. I heard some men keenly resent this order, though bearing without a murmur neglect, fatigue, want, cold, hunger, and nakedness, which they seemed to consider the natural results of war and of the position of a soldier.

The utmost I heard of complaint was in comparing their state with that of their Allies. 'Ah,' they would say, 'they are some centuries before us in everything concerning campaigning; they understand it better.'

But though few possessed a shirt, they resented the order to remove them from the dead.

'I wish we had died up at the Crimea,' I heard one say; 'they did not strip us there. With all the fuss they make about us at home, can they no spare a rag to cover us in the grave? I don't care for a coffin, but to be buried naked like a dog.'

This order was not long enforced. At first each dead body was sewn up in a blanket, but as deaths became numerous and blankets scarce a piece of sacking was used.

My doctor was very liberal as to food and wine, and was found fault with as too liberal. He answered boldly:

'These men are committed to my care; I order what food I think good for them. If I think a man needs a bottle of wine, he shall have it.'

Very soon after he was ordered to the Crimea.

The next, his successor, was young and shy, and did not understand filling up the diet roll, and frequently omitted some men altogether, so the poor fellows had nothing but dry bread. But they bore this trial, like all others, most philo-sophically, or rather most Christianly.

Poor Murphy, now a hungry convalescent, was one of these starvelings, and on my condoling with him on his dinnerless condition, 'Och!' he said, 'I think little of that, my Saviour fasted a good deal longer for me.'

'I'm glad you think of Him,' I said.

''Deed,' he said, 'if it were not for Him, and thinking of Him, I would not get on as I do.'

One day I said to him, 'You have plenty time for prayer now.'

''Deed I have,' he said, 'and shure I should pray for every-body, for everybody is praying for me.' Seeing I looked puzzled, he said, 'You know both the Church of England and of Rome pray daily for the poor soldier—that is for me.'

He used to read his New Testament carefully, but one day, seeing him look disturbed, I said, 'What's the matter?'

'Shure,' he said, 'my priest's a great bigot.'

'Indeed,' I said, 'what do you mean?'

'I had a nice Testament,' he said, 'that my captain gave me, and the priest found me a reading of it, and he took it away.'

I said, 'Perhaps he'll give you another.'

'But it's not another I want,' he said, 'but the very one my captain gave me; I value it for his sake. But I know another priest, a kind man and no bigot, and he is above this one, and I hope to speak to him, and to get it back.'

I never heard if he did. He used to say his mother was a Church of England woman, and his father a Roman Catholic, and he had an equal respect for each, for they were both right in the main.

The private of the 47th who was so kind to Sam Gregg spoke with great regard and respect of his officers. He said they were good religious men, and the colonel like a father to them all. They received Holy Communion before the battle of Alma, in which they suffered severely. This man's colonel and captain were both severely wounded. The colonel before he left the Hospital for home asked to be carried round to take leave of his sick and wounded men. How deeply did the poor men feel such care and kindness, and how it lies in the power of officers to influence their men for good. I never met any so open to kindness and to good influences as these poor sick and wounded men. Oh, that all in authority, especially the officers both of army and navy, would use their talent of influence for the glory of God and for the welfare of the men under their care! Then would our army and navy be indeed invincible, not only against earthly foes, but against spiritual powers of darkness, against impurity and drunkenness. A religious life in an officer, a truly Christian conversation in him, would have far more influence than the stated regular services of the chaplain, valuable as they may be. They are too often taken as matters of course; he is paid to preach and to pray. But in Hospital all religious services, except strictly private ones, were forbidden —all public prayer or preaching. The chaplains were not allowed to have any public services in the wards to avoid giving offence. The only breach of this I knew was on the part of a wounded officer, who went every Sunday and repeated the Litany in several wards. I never heard this complained of, and it was a comfort indeed to many, who told us they would not have known Sunday from week-day but for that. Though the colonel ventured to do this, no chaplain might.

The Irish were in general the most pleasant patients, and the Scotch the least so. Though the real work of the Scotch might have been equal or greater, they had a ruder manner and a mien more grave. I had one Scotch artilleryman who was inclined to grumble at his circumstances, the only patient I ever heard do so, but he had not suffered as most had in the camp.

The half of D Corridor I had was very cold; it faced the north, and several panes of glass were broken, and the orderlies seldom lighted the stoves, and never kept them up. The doctor did not care about a fire, being very quick in moving, and not standing above a few minutes in one place. He did not feel any want of heat, but the poor men lying in a cold draught did. Other nurses and ladies remarked to me the icy breeze which met them in this corridor. Though for many years at home free from chilblains, my hands and feet were here covered with them. Though it was a more than usually severe winter everywhere, the cold here scarcely equalled that of an ordinary winter at home. We had only one fortnight of frost and one fall of snow. In our room at the Barrack Hospital we had no fire or brazier, no curtains or shutters, so that poor Margaret, who at this time still slept there, used to be glad to go straight to bed on returning from her work, about 5 P.M., merely to keep warm. At the General Hospital in our room we had first a charcoal brazier, which was succeeded by a comfortable stove, so that we did not suffer from cold there. But if standing about in D Corridor was trying, and produced chilblains, how much more trying must it have been to the poor men lying in it. Yet I have known poor men, both here and at the Barracks, get out of bed repeatedly and go barefooted along the cold stone floor, even within an hour of death, to avoid troubling the orderlies. One poor young man of the Scots Greys (who was almost devoured by lice) did this eight times the last night of his life. As long as he had strength to move, he said, he would trouble no man. As I tried to free him from his horrid tormentors, 'Ah!' he said, 'what would my poor mother say to see me in this state?'

The Scotch artilleryman from Greenock used to say to me:

'Well, this is a queer Hospital—nothing to eat, nothing to drink—and look there, I never lay in the snow before,' as a few flakes of snow blew in at the window, and rested on his bed. He had been more successful than most in escaping hardships in the Crimea. He had a prejudice against Roman Catholics, and said he did not like to see me so friendly with the nuns, &c.

A tall man of the Scots Greys who lay beside the Oxford lad said to me, after he was gone, 'If there ever was a good, innocent-minded lad, he was one.' Another of the Scots Greys lay on his other side, and the two were seemingly much attached to each other, and wished to go home together, but the younger, named William Donaldson, recovered more quickly, and was sent home before his friend. Donaldson lost his leg in the second Balaclava charge, when the Greys and 1st Royals tried to cover the retreat of the wreck of the Light Brigade. His horse was also disabled, so that it was with great difficulty he got away, trying to crawl with his poor shattered leg. At first looking at his leg, and seeing the flow of blood, he thought in twenty minutes it will all be over, and he lay still, trying to collect his thoughts, and prepare for the great change. Then feeling the blood flowing less rapidly, he looked out for help, and seeing the Duke of Cambridge riding, called out:

'If no one is coming to help me, will your Royal Highness shoot me through the head.'

Soon after some soldiers came and carried him. But his sorrows were not over, for some officers, seeing so many carrying one man, ordered them back to their regiments, and he was left again. At last some Turks came and lifted him so roughly, he fainted, and became unconscious. They took him to the Field Hospital, where his leg was taken off rather high up, and he was carried to the ship and taken to Scutari. On his way to the ship he waved his arm and cried, 'Huzza for Auld Reekie!' He was only eighteen, and seemed to have a robust constitution. He was also cheerful, patient, and sweet-tempered, which contributed to his recovery.

The good Queen's letter[38] was a great comfort to some of the poor men as well as to us. The assurance of her sympathy was deeply valued. Donaldson got a copy of it, and put it over his head, and on my noticing it, he looked up with a sweet expression and said:

'Yes, it's very affecting, and makes our sufferings less to think she cares so for us.'

Burns remarked: 'It's very pleasant and proper, but I hope the good folk at home won't spend all their kindness in words, but will keep it up, and give us enough to keep the pot aboiling when we come back to them. At least,' he added, 'it won't be the Queen's fault, God bless her, if they don't.'

Mrs Bracebridge headed the body of nurses attending Church. One Sunday she rose and left as soon as prayers were over, we all following as in duty bound. A wounded officer limped after us to say the chaplain was about to preach, but though sorry for the mistake, Mrs B. thought it best not to return, so we went to the wards, and the masculine part of the flock had the sermon to themselves for once.

Next to the Scotch artilleryman lay a consumptive patient, a gentle religious lad who, though weak and troubled with a consumptive cough, did not seem to suffer much, and to enjoy a conversation with me. The Scotchman took a tender interest in his consumptive companion who lay beside him. One morning, on entering the ward, I was struck by this lad's altered countenance and difficulty in breathing, and saw that death was approaching. The artilleryman, seeing his friend's state, got up, dressed, and sat by and nursed him to the last.

One very handsome, intelligent, active-minded young man, Sergeant N. of the 1st Royals, asked me one day the meaning of my sleeves, which certainly were of a needless and rather in-convenient length and breadth for nursing.

'Does it mean anything?' he said.

I answered, 'Our dress is a uniform worn by some persons in the Church of England who give themselves to nursing the sick, teaching children, &c.'

'Indeed,' he said, 'I was not aware of any such community. 'I know the Roman Catholics have Sisters of Charity, is it like that? Well,' he said, 'you've told me what I never knew before.'

This young man, who was remarkably handsome and in-telligent, always active and always doing something, had a severe wound in the thigh, but he told me he had interest, and hoped if his wound healed he might get a commission. To his great disappointment, however, he was discharged.

One day, before Sister E.'s dismissal, I met her walking with a lady. As Sister E.'s comrade and co-adjutor, I joined and followed them. She took the lady into her wards, they spoke to some of the men, and there was some difficulty in getting a spoon to divide some jelly she had brought, and the lady seemed distressed at the miserable state of the wards, and the general discomfort. On their leaving I still accompanied them, and something getting wrong about the lady's shoe, she stooped to arrange it. Finding some difficulty, Sister E. also stooped to help, which seemed to distress the lady, who said:

'Oh, don't, Sister, I can't allow you.'

I then offered my services, which were accepted. I understood the lady thought I was of inferior rank, perhaps because Sister E. had a stately commanding presence, and spoke, while I was silent and looked commoner. Soon after the lady left, Sister E. said:

'That was Lady Stratford, wife of the British Ambassador.'

She had met Sister E., and politely said, 'I hope your patients are doing well, Sister?'

'As well as starving, dying men can do,' said Sister E.

'Starving!' said Lady S.; 'what do you mean?'

'Come and see,' said Sister Elizabeth.

Lady S. continued sending us jelly and nice things for the men, but I never again saw her in the wards.

Another evening when I accompanied Sister Elizabeth, an orderly asked her if she would like to see some Russian wounded prisoners. She, supposing them to be privates, answered 'Yes;' and he ushered us into a room in which were three beds, each occupied by a bearded gentleman, who was, we at once understood, a wounded Russian officer. Sister E. offered them some drink from a jug she carried. They accepted it with thanks. She bowed, and we retired. The little conversation on each side was in French. On leaving, Sister E. said to the orderly:

'How could you take us to officers? You may get us into trouble. We are not allowed to attend even our own officers.'

The orderly made our position more ridiculous by putting

his hand on his heart, saying, 'Trust me, madam, I won't betray you.'

One of Margaret's patients said to her, 'Won't I save up and get you a handsome present for all your kindness to me.'

'I don't want any present from you,' M. answered. 'Don't you think Christ can reward me better?'

'Shure, and so He can,' said he, 'if you're contint.'

My doctor often permitted, and even asked me to procure arrowroot or beef-tea for some of the men, but would never sign a requisition. The distress for shirts was still very great, whole wards appearing to be shirtless—at least to possess a shirt was a distinction.

Next day the empty place of the consumptive lad was filled by a lad, a young recruit, a poor ignorant London-bred lad, a pure city arab. Of all religion he seemed utterly ignorant, and equally indifferent. I could not elicit one idea on the subject. He had never been at school—never inside a church—never heard of Christ. I did not meet among Scotch or Irish the dense ignorance and apathy on spiritual matters which was found in some English, both of town and country. He said he never prayed—knew nothing about it. He did not seem very ill at first. One night the orderly asked me to read the directions outside a bottle he was about to administer.

I read, 'Two tablespoonfuls every four hours.'

On his putting these directions into practice by pouring out one tablespoonful and giving it to the patient, his operations were arrested by a yell from the recipient, who started up in bed with a series of screams interspersed with, 'You've killed me! my inside's burnt up! I'm done!'

I went to the sufferer with some barley water, and told the orderly to take the bottle to the dispensary and find out the mistake, and see if it could be rectified. Frightened, and almost crying, he hurried away, while I remained with the lad. The orderly officer passed by, and on my calling his attention to this incident, he merely desired me to continue administering warm barley water, and passed on. Soon after the orderly returned with the young dispenser who had made the mistake, and seemed inclined to laugh at it, and ordered some soothing draught. He said the mixture should have been diluted with eight parts of water, whereas the water was omitted, and that beyond the pain and burning there was no danger. However, in a few days this poor ignorant lad died, his feet and legs turning black some days before the end. I seldom administered medicine, my doctor seldom ordering any, so except cod-liver oil I very seldom had anything to do with medicine.

Towards the end of January our doctor was ordered to the Crimea; his successor was ill of fever; the dresser, a kind, considerate young man, was ill too; and these poor men had only a hurried visit from a doctor who had this duty only for the day, and in addition to his own daily duty. Of course he could take no deep interest in, nor gain much knowledge of these cases, whom he had never seen before, and might never see again.

The Scotch artilleryman was a Presbyterian, and had a Presbyterian dislike to the Church of Rome. One day he said:

'I don't like to see you walking and talking so friendly to those nuns; I don't like them.'

I said, 'I do; they are very kind.'

'Perhaps so,' he said, 'but I don't like their ways. I know we should keep our blessed Lord in continual remembrance—His Cross and Passion, and all He had done and suffered for us should be ever in our hearts, but to wear His graven image dangling by the side, and pulling it about in the hand, is not right or respectful; I don't like it.'

Another Presbyterian (as I came round with some books) said:

'I want none of your books or of your religion—till I get back to my own religion.'

'What is your religion?' I said, expecting to hear of some strange new sect.

'I'm what is called a Protestant Dissenter,' said he.

'Well,' I said, 'you are a Christian; so am I, and I hope our other differences are not so great.'

'Pardon me,' he said, 'there are great differences. You are for general redemption—I am for special election; you are for human frailty—I am for total and utter depravity; you say Christ died for all—I say, He died only for His chosen;' and he ran on with a fluent enumeration of differences, the discussion of which seemed to me very undesirable, so I left him in a triumphant exposition of his theological principles. He said his father was a Presbyterian divine. Though ready for polemic discussion, he seemed a wild, reckless fellow, whose religion little touched his heart or influenced his life. He was shot in the back—a few hairbreadths the doctor said would have made his wound fatal. He said he would never write home—if he lived, his friends would see him walk in some day; and if he died, they might find out as they chose; he would never bother them with letters. He told me he refused to attend the Church of England, and had often preferred being sent to the black hole till he stirred up other Dissenters in his regiment, so that all objected to go to church, and at last gained their point.

The kindness of the men to each other was in general great. Aslett in his deepest sufferings—and I believe they were beyond conception—ever had thought and feeling for his comrades. Though expressing little of religious feeling himself, if he saw any one near death he was anxious and restless till a clergyman came to see him; and though oppressed with weakness and pain, not able to raise himself on his hard pillow, he still tried to exert himself on behalf of others.

Many of the doctors not understanding the complicated diet roll,[39] found filling them up a perplexing task, and their frequent mistakes caused suffering to the poor patients. The patients on extras, those who were weakest and needed most frequent support, had frequently to wait from an early breakfast of dry bread and tea at 8 A.M. till nightfall without food. Several told me they felt hungry about noon, but before dinner came at 4 P.M. they were faint with want, and had no appetite. I heard my doctor complain of this to the head surgeon, who said it should be rectified, but it was not in my time. In some cases the effects of this long fast were very trying, and I used to smuggle in trifling assistance in some cases, though it was little I could do. At my own means I used to save a little bread and butter and meat, and make some sandwiches, and gave them to the most needy after their wounds were dressed. I believe this helped in some cases to sustain life. Of course if the diet roll had been carefully arranged by the doctors, and their orders carefully fulfilled, any interference by the nurses would have been unnecessary and undesirable. But in some cases they were quite unable to endure a long fast, and this little supply seemed useful. I gave it only to those in greatest need, and I never found this created the slightest jealousy. They seemed rather glad and thankful for each other. In hospitals at home I have met cases of jealousy. But from whatever cause, these men seemed to me more noble, patient, generous, and unselfish than human nature generally is. I trust their sufferings were really sanctified—that Christ was with them and in them, or they could not have been so far like Him.

One poor patient would take nothing but what I prepared. He had no appetite, and refused to eat, but one day he said to me:

'I have a few things under my bed, perhaps if you made me something with them I could eat it.'

I found in an old shoe two eggs and some other material, and carrying them off, composed some little mess he pronounced 'beautiful.' I did this for him and some others. Many could not eat the food prepared in the General Hospital kitchen. The puddings were made of stiff rice unwashed, and so intermingled with chaff and stones as to be quite unfit for the sick and dying. The men never grumbled at their food but it was often rejected when a little care and trouble in cooking it might have made it acceptable. The arrowroot was brought up in pewter soup plates, made very stiff, and sweetened with coarse dark sugar. It was frequently laid on the bed beside men who were in a state of stupor or exhaustion, unconscious of its presence, and even if conscious quite unable to sit up and feed themselves, so it lay for about twenty minutes, when the orderly came to carry it away and devour it himself, or give it to some voracious convalescent. I have heard of an orderly eating six or seven portions of patients who had rejected it. Yet all these men needed their arrowroot, and if gently roused and fed, scarcely one would have rejected it. I did what I could in feeding the worst cases, but it was a slow operation, and before I had time to feed more than two men it grew so cold as to be unpalatable.

During January I heard that a nurse was coming to the long neglected corridor through which I daily passed, and very thankful I felt, for they needed care which the wild rough boys who acted as orderlies were little able to give. I knew these men by sight as well as my own, and marked the frequent changes there made by death. The first patient in the corridor was a very handsome young lancer, wounded in three places at Balaclava. I knew well his sweet innocent face; he died at last. Another man I watched sinking day by day, most gentle patient he was; and I grew so accustomed to his pale, wasted, deathly countenance, that when one morning, looking for him in his usual place, I saw his bed empty, it was almost as much a shock as if I had no reason to expect it. It seemed a common occurrence in this corridor and the adjoining wards for a man to be found dead, neither orderly nor patient in the next bed being aware of it. Mrs B., a most kind and indefatigable nurse, was put on duty here, and it was delightful to see and hear her motherly kindness to these poor men. 'But they *would* die in spite of her,' she said, as deaths continued frequent. She seemed to feel it a personal affront that, notwithstanding all her tender watchful care, her spoonfuls of jelly and beef-tea, her petting and motherly coaxing, the men were perversely and obstinately bent on evading her endeavours and defying her entreaties, and *would* die. She got excited in her vain efforts to prolong life.

'I gave him four spoonfuls of jelly, and he looked up in my face and died. Four spoonfuls!' she repeated.

But in some cases her jelly and beef-tea may have been useful; and even if not, still dying faces would light up with grateful recognition at her coaxing words:

'Come, try to take a little, just to please your own old nursie; you'll take one spoonful.' It was a long time since the poor fellows had heard such words. And she did check the careless neglect of the boys who acted as orderlies. It cheered me to see her comely face and hear her kind words in these neglected parts, and to think that now no poor fellow would die there utterly neglected, and no doubt it cheered them still more.

A new arrangement was made about this time. It was that each lady or sister should not so much nurse actually herself, but have two nurses under her to superintend in one division of the Hospital. I very much preferred remaining where I was, and with my old patients, whom I would have been sorry to leave, and some of whom would have been sorry to lose me. Miss N. very kindly granted my request, and indeed in all my personal intercourse with her the impression she gave me at first of kindness, firmness, and wisdom was fully realized. I was about to learn her value in a deeper degree, to know how dear she was to the sick, how her sweet voice and gentle words could cheer and soothe the heart when sinking in that most depressing fever, sickness.

I used to feel now daily more weak and weary. For change I used at times to go out and sit in the Cemetery, to see if the air would revive me; but whether the country was really getting into a pestilential state, or that my sensations were becoming morbidly acute, I found so many revolting objects, I was glad to retire, more sick and tired than when I went out. We seemed constantly stumbling on dead dogs and cattle, open drains, &c. The whole country seemed to me to be becoming pestiferous. One day I went out with Miss Smythe (who went afterwards to Kulilee, where she died of fever), and after trying different pathways to escape these sickening objects on our return, we watched at a distance our soldiers' funeral. No longer borne each, as they used to be, by four of their comrades, nor by Turks, who succeeded them, they seemed all taken in one cart, as in the plague of London in 1665, or in the beginning of the cholera visitation at Plymouth in 1849. We were not near enough to observe details; some of the nurses who went nearer were shocked.

We also met a body of convalescents about to return to the Crimea, but their pale faces and frequent cough seemed to proclaim them unfit at least for Crimean service. At this time mortality was at its height. Yet the places of the dead were immediately refilled, so that the Hospitals remained full to overcrowding, and the Hospital at Kulilee was opened and began to fill. The Hospitals were overcrowded, fever increasing fast and spreading; doctors, chaplains, nurses, and more than all, orderlies, were attacked by it, and some died. The poor orderlies had little chance of escape. Confined to the crowded wards day and night, employed in carrying away the dead and in all the most trying parts of nursing, and *expected* to sit up every third night—though I believe very few did so—they lay down in their clothes, and fell so fast asleep that no appeal could rouse them.

Night nursing was much wanted, but with our limited number and want of place of retirement, it was impossible to do much in that way. One very good and zealous doctor often requested us to sit up with, or at least to visit occasionally during the night, some of his men he was anxious about and who should receive food frequently, and we did so, sitting up in our own room, and every twenty minutes or so sallying out with a little food to visit our patients. There was something very sad and striking in these silent walks through long lanes of our brave sick and dying countrymen, all sunk in deep repose, save here and there some weary wakeful patients would look up at us and ask for relief or for a word of sympathy. But in general deathlike silence prevailed in the ward while we passed, as gently as we could, to our appointed task along the dimly lighted corridors. One night eight were mentioned, and Miss Anderson and I agreed to sit up the first half of the night, and then to call two others to take our place for the last part. But there was no need for doing so—before the first half of the night all had died. We spent a few hours in trying to soothe their dying hours, going from one deathbed to another, and when all were at rest we returned to our quarters and went to bed.

My men were kind and sympathising to each other, though sometimes, when a dying man was restless and noisy, they would complain; but when their poor noisy comrade was still in death they seemed to repent, and would say, 'Poor fellow, he could not help it.' It is in such scenes the value of the Cross is felt; the length, and breadth, and height, and depth of the love of God in Christ outstretching and sheltering the depth of human sin and suffering, making the dark and dreary grave a sweet cave of shelter from the cruel storms of life. The Queen's message[40] of sympathy and care, the thought of her royal heart beating and bleeding for her faithful suffering troops, cheered many a sinking heart; but it needed a Royal message from the King of kings, the Conqueror of sin and death and hell, to cast a light over the dark valley the poor sufferers were passing through, and to make them more than conquerors over the last enemy through their great Captain, who loved them and gave Himself for them. Yes, faithful soldiers of our Queen and country, who counted not your young lives cut short too high a price for their honour and safety, who bore uncomplainingly neglect and hunger and cold and want in reward of your faithful service, and never murmured as a slow and lingering death closed at once your service and your sufferings, it was He who bore our griefs and carried our sorrows who enabled you so to act, His Cross upheld, His grace supported, His mercy encompassed and received you.

In the General Hospital we had two large rooms, one for

the Anglican sisters and ladies, and another for the nurses, and a smaller one for the nuns. Sister Bertha, Margaret, and I were the Anglicans; Miss Anderson, Miss Smythe, Miss Tebbut the secular ladies. In this one room, which was large and airy, we slept, lived, ate, had prayers, received visitors, and performed all the duties of life, kept stores, and cooked. So we *all* felt we *must* keep well; in such circumstances to be ill and confined to bed was indeed not to be thought of—it would be a capital crime against decency and order. In this conviction I struggled on, weak and weary, but hoping it would pass off, and cheered by seeing my men recovering. We rose about daybreak, Margaret generally first, and swept the room. Then we tidied and aired the room, made our beds, and had breakfast. One of us remained to wash up and give out stores, while the rest proceeded to the wards. If there were any particular need, we visited the wards before breakfast, but we generally found such confusion, such commingling of dust and smoke, wards being swept and stoves lighted, that we found a speedy retreat advisable. This ordeal must have been trying to the consumptive patients. The floors were paved with stone, which seemed of a soft crumbling nature, so that sweeping created quantities of dust.

One day about the end of February or beginning of March, feeling more unwell than usual, I spent some hours lying on the floor, though I made an effort to reach the Barrack Hospital. On the road in returning I met Dr O'., who told me I looked ill, and bid me take care of myself. That night we were engaged to receive Holy Communion with a poor dying soldier. That time was chosen as the tumult and distractions of the day were over, and the calm of night allowed the celebration of the Holy Communion to be offered without the irreverence which must have occurred while the business of the day was going on. Indeed, all the circumstances made the commemoration of our Lord's death and the reception of His sacrament very sacred and touching. The hushed silence, the dim light cast upon dying faces, made the words of the service fall with deep impressiveness; it seemed to cast the light of our dying Saviour's deathless love across the dark pathway of His suffering followers. But that night we were disappointed; the chaplain was too ill to come, so after waiting some time, on receiving a message to that effect, we left the ward and retired to bed. Next morning I felt too ill to rise, and when about to make a second attempt, Dr O'Flaherty came in and forbade it. Soon after I became too ill to be conscious of anything but great pain in the head, noise and deafness. I was conscious too of much kindness from Miss Tebbut, Margaret, and Miss Nightingale when she came to see me. Miss Tebbut was a Unitarian in creed, but as Margaret sometimes said, 'the unbeliever is the best Christian in the room'. She put on leeches on my head, but not being accustomed to such, and having a great aversion to them, she asked for a nurse to help her; but on Mrs C. saying, 'Folk should never begin what they are afraid to finish,' she dispensed with assistance and finished her job well.

I felt the danger and inconvenience I was inflicting on my companions, and wished to be removed. I believe the bad air of the Hospital, fatigue, and mental anxiety caused this illness, and that it was not contagious. No one in the room took it, though my being so ill among them must have been disagreeable. They expected my death. A nurse afterwards told me that for ten days or a fortnight, every morning they expected to hear that I was gone, and she described me as 'the lady that *would* not die'. It was very much like though worse than the fever I had five years before after nursing nearly four months in the Cholera Hospitals in Plymouth. A young doctor in the room above me died of fever during my illness, and also one of the kindest and best of the nurses also died of the same soon after. A nurse chosen to attend these cases was full of hope and enthusiasm. On hearing she was appointed to this duty, she danced round the room, saying:

'I'll bring him round, see if I don't bring him round,' and clapping her hands.

I was ill in bed, though no longer deaf, and I said:

'Don't boast; life and death are not in your hands, though you are a good nurse.'

When both her patients died, I heard she was so disappointed she wished to go home.

Miss Nightingale promised to have me moved as soon as I was able.

One day, when lying alone, I felt my bed shake and rock under me, and looking up, saw the room and everything in it rocking. I knew at once it was an earthquake, and expected to see the roof fall, and to be swallowed; but though it was an awful expectation, I had no fear. I only thought wars, rumours of wars, earthquakes, surely the end is coming. The shaking continued some time, then all was still. On some one coming into the room I said:

'We've had an earthquake.'

They afterwards told me it created great fear in the wards, that all out of bed, and many who had been confined to bed, rushed out of doors; many who had shown no emotion in battle were crying and trembling, and left the bed to which they had been confined though too feeble to return unassisted. One, I was told, leapt from a window and was killed. Miss N. told me many minarets in Constantinople had been thrown down, and that in a Greek town many had been killed and wounded.

Soon after this Miss N. had me moved to the Barrack Hospital. I was still too weak and ill to know or care much about it. Margaret afterwards told me it had been arranged some Turkish porters were to carry me, but she begged so earnestly that I might have soldiers of our army, she got that granted, and Miss Nightingale brought four soldiers, who lifted my mattress on a stretcher such as was used for removing the dead. I was quite sensible, and I did not know where I was going, but was quite content and happy, and felt the fresh breeze of the open air and the beautiful scenery very refreshing as I was being conveyed to the Barrack Hospital. I was carried in at the

Sultan's gate, and then upstairs to our old quarters, the big tower room. Here, though I steadily recovered and gained strength, my worst sufferings began. With returning powers came increasing anxiety and grief, fear of being sent home, and so never being allowed to return to my patients, and my fears were realised. Dr. C [Cumming] came and spoke of my going home. This always raised a tumult and fever in mind and body, and as he came frequently and spoke of my return, I said at last I felt too ill to move, and would not consent to do so. After this his visits were discontinued. I continued gaining strength, and began to rise and walk. Mrs Bracebridge took me out, and one day I went with her to the stores, and saw the havoc rats were making. Among the stores I found a barrel of wine directed to me. Another day I was allowed to visit my patients. Some were gone, others hoping soon to return to their duty in the Crimea—all welcomed gladly my return, and I began to hope I might soon be allowed to do so. But Dr M'. [McGrigor] came in one day and said I must go home. As he had spoken of my returning to my duty in the wards, I was much disappointed, and I suppose showed it as he said my health required a change, and if I were his own sister he would order it, but if the war continued he would send for me. He died himself next autumn. Soon after I was told to make ready for my return. I put the little I wanted into a bag. A big boxful of things was pressed on me, but as I did not think they belonged to me, I steadily declined its company, saying *I would not* have it.

Mrs B. [Bull], a widow lady, who had nursed in the corridor next mine, and had afterwards gone up to the Crimea, had an interview with Lord Raglan, and returned to Constantinople with Miss L. [Langston] (who was thought to be dying of fever) and Miss E. The captain of the ship which brought them from Balaclava at first refused to take a dying lady, but he was at last induced to receive her, though it was feared she would die. There was a storm in the Black Sea, in which Miss L. was rolled out of bed. But this rough treatment seemed to bring a reaction, she began to rally, and though still very ill, arrived at Constantinople in a much less hopeless condition than that in which she had left the Crimea. Lord Napier[41] had kindly offered to receive those sick ladies into his house in Constantinople, but there was no one at the landing place to receive them or show them the way to Lord Napier's, so they remained tossing in the open boat till an officer asked them if he could in any way assist them. Miss Erskine said she wanted some conveyance to take the sick lady she was with to Lord Napier's. He went away, but returned with some soldiers, who lifted the stretcher and mattress on which Miss L. lay, and carried her to Lord Napier's, Miss E. accompanying her, but leaving Mrs B. alone with the luggage on the pier. Mrs B. was recovering from a slight attack of fever, and found her situation too trying. Turks, Greeks, and dogs were crowding round, all jabbering, vociferating, and yelping, and all utterly unintelligible to the poor lady left in charge, so she began to call aloud for 'Help! help! for a poor English lady, widow of a British officer who lay in Spain between two general officers!'

The doleful outcry reached a man-of-war, and the captain sent a boat to inquire into the matter. Learning what they could from the agitated lady, who feared being thrust into the sea, and the luggage she had in charge made a prey, the officer of the boat told his men to take the lady and luggage to the ship, and said to Mrs B. the captain would settle the matter. On hearing particulars, the captain ordered some of the sailors to carry the luggage, and see the lady safe to Lord Napier's, which was done.

Hearing that Mrs B. was to return with me, I went over with a lady to Constantinople to see her and Miss Langston. Crossing in a caique was very pleasant, the views beautiful, the conveyance luxurious. We found Miss L. getting better, and Mrs B. recovered from her fright, but subject to feverish attacks. A few days after I was allowed to visit my old wards. I found some, not many, had died, a few returned to Sebastopol, and some gone home, and a good many fresh cases come from the Crimea. I was glad to see my old friends, and I think they were glad to see me. Murphy said he had prayed for me; another said he had missed me much, and asked daily when I was to return. I did not tell him I was to be sent home, and never return—never know what became of these brave patient Christlike men.

At the pier I found the box I had repudiated, standing as if it were determined to accompany me, but on my repeating my determination that it should not do so, and that if it went I would not, it was left standing in solitary state. Its ultimate fate I never learnt. Next day I went on board *Le Gange*, which was a French ship, though built on the Clyde, and first called the *Black Swan*. A number of French invalid soldiers were being sent home in it. There were also a few British officers, a Queen's messenger, an American lady and gentleman, a French family, and a good many French officers. I was glad to see our officers were not only the tallest, finest-looking men on board, but that they seemed the kindest—the quickest to sympathise with all sufferers. The French soldier's food seemed poor and squalid compared with our best cabin meals. One of the French brought his share to show to one of the French officers, complaining of the small quantity. The French officer merely shrugged his shoulders. One of ours, overhearing the complaint, ran down to the state cabin, where dinner was being laid, and seizing a loaf, gave it to the soldier who had complained.

In the evening as we steamed away and night came on, we looked back to the great Hospital, and saw lights glimmering through the wards. How I envied those we left still ministering to the sick and suffering. Our voyage would have been pleasant but for the evident suffering of the poor invalid French soldiers, and the knowledge that several died, and every night some bodies were committed to the deep. One morning before rising the engine ceased to work, and the ship stood still. I dressed quickly went on deck, and saw a little boat was rowing about as if seeking something. An American passenger, who seemed a religious teacher, came to me and said:

'The poor fellow is gone, they can't find him.'

I asked, 'Whom do they seek.'

He said, 'One of the French soldiers threw himself over-board, and the captain sent a boat to see if he could be rescued, but in vain.'

The seekers and the boat returned to the ship, and the engines began to work, and we were soon far from the place. It seems the poor man had announced his purpose to his comrades, and was not persuaded to forego it, nor did its execution seem to cause much sensation.

The Mediterranean was for the most part beautifully calm on this return voyage. Miss Nightingale bid us call at Athens to meet and come home with Miss Stanley,[42] so Mrs Bull and I landed at Pirius [Piraeus], and went in a pretty pony phaeton to Athens with some letters of introduction, but find-ing Miss Stanley had not come, and that no one knew when she was expected, we thought it best to return as quickly as possible to catch our ship and continue our journey by it. We reached it just in time. The country was beautiful, and the city deeply interesting, but we had little time to examine or enjoy them.

On the voyage a number of pretty little birds lighted on the ship, seeming so weary and exhausted that they allowed the sailors to take them in their hands. Our good officers would not allow any one to hurt them, but gave them food and water and a sleeping-place in their berth, and let them fly next morning. It was pleasant to see men who had suffered, and seen such sufferings as they had, yet anxious to relieve the sufferings and supply the wants of these helpless little wanderers. We passed through the Straits of Messina and saw Mount Etna, and in two days after reached Marseilles. The French soldiers who were able seemed to take pains to be clean and tidy on landing. Some were too ill for the effort, and a few were dying. One who seemed very far gone lay on deck, his head resting on his knapsack. Col. J. tried to procure a softer pillow for him, but it seemed in vain.

Mrs B. and I went to the hotel, and while sitting there a gentleman came up to us, and in a kind English voice and tongue asked if he could be of any use. I recognised him as the doctor who had attended Holy Communion regularly, and we gladly accepted his (Dr Smyth, of Leeds) kind offer of travelling with us and assisting us any way he could. As both Mrs B. and I were still weak, and I spoke French with difficulty, and Mrs B. not at all, his presence and company were the greatest help and comfort, and he treated us with most Christian kindness, and turned a journey I dreaded into one of ease and pleasure. He managed everything for us.

The first night on the train was close, and we were rather crowded, some nuns and children being in the same carriage. The nuns said their prayers before we started without any symptom either of ostentation or of false shame, but just as an obvious duty, and then composed themselves to sleep. But the heat and closeness caused thirst and disturbed sleep, so at every station a cry for water rose, and the nuns responded, '*De l'eau! de l'eau!*' and our kind doctor and a young companion he had picked up sprang out of the carriage to satisfy our thirst, but they had no vessel but one shell which scarcely held a wine-glassful, and before it could be replenished the train had to move, and the poor sufferers had to endure. However, some passengers in the next carriage, hearing our distress, lent us a saucepan which held enough for the whole party, and was thankfully passed round.

On reaching Paris we spent two days there, and then went on to Boulogne and thence to London. Here our kind doctor left us, and I drove to Osnaburg Street Home.

POSTSCRIPT—BALMORAL

Undoubtedly the most memorable event in Sarah Anne's declining years was her visit to Balmoral Castle in 1897 to be presented with the Royal Red Cross by Queen Victoria. In this Diamond Jubilee year, the surviving four members of the Bermondsey contingent of Sisters of Mercy also received the Royal Red Cross. They were decorated at Windsor in June. Sister Mary Aloysius, too, was decorated but, at the age of 76, felt too frail to travel and received her medal by post in her native Ireland. Sarah Anne was thus the only surviving Anglican Sister of Florence Nightingale's original party to be decorated by the Queen. The account that follows was written by Charles Terrot's great grandmother, Sarah Anne's cousin, Alice Terrot, who accompanied her.

Edinburgh, Tuesday October 26th. Off to the station. There met Sarah Anne, her sister, Lizzie, her niece Annie Malcolm and her friend Miss Bruce. Lizzie only came to see us off. Reached Aberdeen for luncheon, then took the train for Ballater [the nearest station to Balmoral which is about nine miles away]. When we arrived at Ballater, we were trotted off to the village where lodgings had been secured for us by Miss Bruce.

Things were a trifle primitive but we were in the humour for liking everything. All was as Scotch as were the Highlands and we were going to see the Queen. So we were most contented and very happy.

Ballater and Balmoral, Wednesday October 27th. Awoke this morning with brilliant sunshine bursting in on me to usher in the eventful day. No bells in the cottage, but we got a tiny jug of warm water. We put Miss Nightingale's assurance into practice that one can wash as well in a teacupful of water, as in a big bath.

By and by came the ceremonies of the Toilette. Sarah Anne looked very sweet and dignified and every inch a lady in all her beautiful simplicity. All new—black of course—white strings to her bonnet, and for this occasion a little white lace in front—white kid gloves.

A nice landau, ordered by Miss Bruce, came to the door. Two horses and a driver are always ordered for Balmoral. The day was perfect—not a cloud—an Italian sky. The extraordinary beauty of the scenery was enhanced by the brilliant sunshine. We hardly spoke—I wished to keep my dear Cousin very quiet. [Sarah Anne and Alice were now travelling on their own.]

Before entering the Castle grounds, a person came forward to ask me to inscribe our names. I replied 'We are invited', so he bowed and let us proceed. We passed beneath a beautiful archway remaining from the Jubilee, which was made of Everlastings—'WELCOME' outside, and the same inside but in Gaelic.

On arriving at the Castle, I asked the footman if I was to send in my card. He said, 'Oh no! Sir Arthur Bigg [the Lord Chamberlain] told me you were coming.'

We passed through long corridors, then upstairs, all carpeted with crimson. We were shown into a room which was a combination of bedroom and sitting-room. In the middle was a writing-table with every requisite but quite plain paper and quill pens. When we had been there a few minutes, one of the Maids of Honour, Miss Bulteel, came in and talked a little, very pleasantly, telling us the news had just arrived of the death of the Duchess of Teck. Then she asked us if we would like to go into the Household Drawing-room.

We went along more corridors and found ourselves in a lovely room carpeted with the Royal Hunting Stuart. She said, 'We are very proud of our view,' and it certainly was quite perfect with the flower garden in the foreground.

We sat and talked, then came in an old gentleman whom she introduced as 'the Duke of Richmond'. So the Lords and Ladies kept coming in one by one, and then we went into luncheon, Lady Ampthill [Senior Lady-in-Waiting] leading the way. On entering the dining-room, Mr. Ponsonby [Gold Rod] came forward and greeted us most kindly and with great courtesy. He was Host.

We sat down 15. First soup, then croquettes served on a pile of fried parsley. Another entrée with potato chips— Roast grouse—Roast lamb—potatoes, spinach, peas and cabbage. The main dishes were served on solid gold plates which I was told dated back to Charles II.

Brown bread pudding with a solid cream sauce, and jelly. Delicious butter stamped with the Royal Crown—Pears and Grapes. Claret or Moselle. I chose the latter—it was excellent. We were waited upon by four tall footmen in scarlet and gold livery, and a Butler.

I sat next to Dr. Woods, a Naval man [a physician to the Queen]—we became good friends and I told him about my dear brother Willie having been in the Queen's Yacht because he had been so brave and how good he was and how he died. Also I told him about dear Dirk [a young nephew, in the Navy] and what a wonderful examination he had passed. 'Oh,' he said, 'it is rare thing to do THAT!' He promised to look in the Navy List, and there see it all. Altogether it was most delightful.

I did not feel a bit nervous but as cool and calm as possible which was the better for dear Sarah Anne. Coffee was served in the Drawing-Room.

[Here Alice omitted mention of what happened next:

Sarah Anne, who had only toyed with her food at lunch and refused wine, became rather emotional, vividly remembering her departed comrades and favourite patients at Scutari: Elizabeth, Clara, Sister Mary de Gonzaga, Sister Jean Chantel, Margaret, Ethelreda, the rumbustious Mrs. Clarke, Tom Burns, Aslett, Murphy, Dr. Maclean, Dr. O'Flaherty and doubtless many others.

For a few moments it seemed possible that the investiture would have to be called-off—especially in view of the fact that the Queen herself was much disturbed by the news of the Duchess of Teck. Then a maid of honour, a rather pretty fair-haired young girl, Miss Bulteel, took charge of the situation. She guided Sarah Anne into a corner of the drawing-room, and told her gently that the other Scutari nurses were being thought of by the Queen and she *must* go through with the ceremony as a tribute to the memory of them all. Meanwhile, everyone else in the room—except for Alice—pretended not to notice Sarah Anne's very understandable distress.

Then came the summons to meet her Sovereign.

Sarah Anne stood up, straightened the little bit of white lace on the front of her dress, smiled bravely at Alice, and the two old ladies were ushered out of the drawing-room by Lady Ampthill.—C.T.]

With Sarah Anne leaning on my arm, we passed down a long corridor. It was evident at once which was the door of the Queen's Apartment, for there stood two Indians, two big footmen, a stalwart Highlander and a Master of Ceremonies. Lady Ampthill went in and returned saying the Queen was not quite ready and we must wait a few minutes and sit down. She returned again and we followed her.

She said, 'First make your curtseys, then if the Queen puts out her hand, kiss it—if not, do nothing.'

I took in Sarah Anne leaning on my arm.

We made our curtseys very nicely, then I pushed Sarah Anne forward. The Queen put forward her hand and the Heroine kissed it. The Queen sat so very low that Sarah Anne had a difficulty in rising. The Queen said 'Raise her up,' but she got up without help. The Queen looked so benign—so gracious. She smiled the whole time, not a bit like the photographs which are grave. She took a case off the little table by her side and said to Lady Ampthill, 'Pin it on.' Then when done, she handed the case to Lady Ampthill and I took it.

The Queen asked Sarah Anne a few questions about the work she had done and if she had worked in any hospital on her return from Scutari. S.A. replied so faintly that I answered for her: 'St. Thomas's Hospital, Madam.' The Queen said a few kind words, smiled very sweetly, and bowed to us both when we retired, sidling away as well as we could arm-in-arm.

We then returned to the drawing-room where the Lords and Ladies were assembled and all anxious to see the Decoration. A gentleman, who had charge of the Queen's Birthday Book, said the Queen wished us to write our names in it. Sarah Anne made a blot. I am glad to say I did not.

And then all was over and our carriage was announced.

*   *   *

In her old age, Sarah Anne's mind often wandered back to the days of nursing in Scutari and she would speak in the most graphic way, almost as though the events narrated in her Journal had only recently occurred.

She died peacefully, by all accounts seeming to think she was back in her room at the Barrack Hospital.

NOTES & REFERENCES

SETTING THE SCENE pp. 13–63

1 Russell was the correspondent of the London *Times* in the Crimea. He was the first of the modern breed of war correspondents.

2 This was not true. Female nurses had been employed on the wards of military hospitals since these first appeared in 1690. They were usually soldiers' wives and served in general hospitals, regimental hospitals, flying (or field) hospitals or whatever they were called at the time. During the Peninsular war women ceased to be employed as nurses but continued as cooks and washerwomen. In 1832 women were no longer employed in regimental hospitals in any capacity.

3 Woodham-Smith, p. 137.

4 Director General's Precis of Letters, vol. I, pp. 158–160. (Cantlie, vol. 2, p. 67.)

5 Cantlie, vol. 2, p. 97.

6 Director General's Precis of Letters, vol. I, p. 277. (Cantlie, vol. 2, p. 131.)

7 *Nova et Vetera*. 'Letters from the Crimea.' *British Medical Journal*, 2, 1103. 1954.

8 *Report [of the Commission] upon the State of the Hospitals of the British Army in the Crimea and Scutari*, p. 321.

II

9 *Selected Writings of Florence Nightingale*. See 'Subsidiary notes as to the introduction of female nursing into military hospitals.' 1858.

10 See note 9.

11 (A) Lady Volunteer, vol. 1, p. 4. (The Lady Volunteer was Frances Magdalen Taylor who went out to Scutari in the second party under Mary Stanley.)

12 Director General's Precis of Letters, vol. I, p. 159. (Cantlie, vol. 2, p. 91.)

13 A letter written to Parthenope, Lady Verney, in July 1855. (Woodham-Smith, p. 237.)

Notes & References

III

14 Goodman, Margaret. 1862.
15 Goodman, Margaret. 1862.
16 Goodman, Margaret. 1863.
17 Goodman, Margaret. 1863.
18 The Tractarians were followers of Pusey, Keble, Newman, and their like—the Oxford movement. Their objective was to assert the authority of the Anglican Church.
19 From a letter written to Margaret Goodman (1863).
20 Goodman, Margaret. 1863.

IV

21 The functions of the different types of military hospitals, their origins, and their distinctions are described on pages 37–41. In the present context the term 'general hospital' always refers to a military general hospital; civilian hospitals did not enter the picture at all.
22 *Medical and Surgical History of the British Army in the War against Russia 1854–6*, vol. 1, Preface. London; Harrison. 1858.
23 In his evidence to the Hospitals Commission, Menzies said 'I have followed the general rules for regimental hospitals, so far as I could.' *Report [of the Commission] upon the State of the Hospitals of the British Army in the Crimea and Scutari*, p. 305.
24 Percy. *Journal des Campagnes du Baron Percy Chirurgien en chef de la Grande Armée (1754–1825)*. Introduction by M. É. Longin. 2nd ed., p. 16. Paris; Plon-Nourrit. 1904.
25 The titles given to the ranks in the Army Medical Department had varied through the years, though by 1840 they had become standardized. Nevertheless, practice was slipshod and obsolete titles such as inspector of hospitals continued to be used even in official documents.
26 Nightingale, Florence. *Notes on Nursing. What it is and what it is not*, p. 23, footnote. London; Harrison, 1860.
27 *Les Sépulchres de la Grande Armée, ou Tableau des Hôpitaux Pendant la Dernière Campagne de Bonaparte*. Paris; Eymery. 1813. (By an anonymous author.)
28 (A) Lady Volunteer, vol. 1, pp. 73–77.
29 Cantlie, vol. 2, pp. 117, 174, 183.
30 *Selected Writings of Florence Nightingale*. See 'Subsidiary notes as to the introduction of female nursing into military hospitals.' 1858.
31 Pirogoff was the leading Russian surgeon of his day. Although a civilian, he saw a great deal of military service and during the campaign in

the Caucasus in 1847 had been the first man to use ether anaesthesia (discovered the previous year) on the battlefield.

32 Garrison, F. H. *Notes on the History of Military Medicine*. Washington; Association of Military Surgeons. 1922. (See pp. 171–172.)

33 See note 32.

V

34 Medical comforts were for the most part extras to a soldier's very basic ration. They included port wine, brandy, sherry, preserved meats, meat essences, sago, arrowroot, rice, oatmeal, dried vegetables and potatoes, turtle soup, calf's foot jelly, concentrated milk, tea, sugar, cocoa, and also soap.

35 Quoted from Alexander W. Kinglake's *Invasion of the Crimea*. Smith's actual words before the Roebuck Committee (*Reports from the Select Committee on the Army before Sebastopol*, First and Second Reports, 8064, p. 397) were rather more prosaic but their message was the same.

36 *Reports from the Select Committee on the Army before Sebastopol*, Third Report, 16447–9, p. 274.

37 *Report of the Commissioners Appointed to Inquire into the Regulations Affecting the Sanitary Condition of the Army, the Organization of Military Hospitals, and the Treatment of the Sick and Wounded*, Appendix LXXIX, Letter No. 18, p. 7.

38 *Reports from the Select Committee on the Army before Sebastopol*, Third Report, 16558, p. 279.

39 Pringle, J. *Observations on the Diseases of the Army*, 3rd ed. London; Millar, Wilson, Durham, and Payne. 1761. (First edition, 1752.)

SARAH ANNE'S JOURNAL pp. 65–164

1 Margaret Goodman. She was a special friend of Sarah Anne's. She was one of only two Sellonite Sisters who went to the Crimea itself and remained there until the end of the war. In 1862 she wrote an account of her experiences and, a year later, a book on Sisterhoods in the Church of England which was concerned mainly with the Sellonites.

2 The London headquarters of the Sellonites and the St. Saviour's Sisterhood was in Osnaburg Street (now in N.W.1, and spelt Osnaburgh).

3 Elizabeth Wheeler. Her letter home which her relatives sent to *The Times* for publication created a furore as Sarah Anne mentions later in her journal. (See pp. 127–8.)

Notes & References

4 The original Louise Marie de Gonzaga, daughter of the Duke of Modena, was a Queen of Poland. She had been brought up at the French court where she had been one of St. Vincent de Paul's Ladies. In 1652 she asked that three of his Sisters of Charity should be sent to Poland.

5 *Vectis* was built for speed to carry the mail between Marseilles and Malta. The owners had difficulty getting crews as, even in tolerable weather, the bunks were constantly saturated with spray.

6 Mrs. Hodges died at Scutari of a 'fever'.

7 The Bracebridges were great travellers. Mr. Bracebridge had taken part in the Greek fight for independence from the Turks.

8 Mrs. Clarke. She had been Florence Nightingale's housekeeper at the Institution for the Care of Sick Gentlewomen in Distressed Circumstances at 1 Upper Harley Street.

9 Negus is port or sherry, taken in hot water and sweetened or spiced. It was much in demand as a medical comfort at Scutari.

10 The actual room in the quarters given to Miss Nightingale where the Russian general died was that allocated to the Sellonites. Margaret Goodman tells us that his white hairs were still scattered about.

11 'No painting, however graphic,' wrote Miss Grace Ramsay in *Memoir of Bishop Grant,* 'could convey a true idea of what they one and all endured in their self-imposed warfare with sickness and death—in the stinging cold, when everything was frozen, without a fire, food scanty, and so bad as to reduce them to a choice between sickness and hunger. During the first six weeks a drink of pure water was a luxury not to be had!'

Sarah Anne later commented: 'This seems to me a rather exaggerated description!'

12 Staff Surgeon First Class McGrigor, the superintendent of the Barrack Hospital. He was a popular and respected man. He died of cholera in November 1855 while still superintendent.

13 In her evidence to the Hospitals Commission (p. 331), Florence Nightingale described how the nurses were allocated to the wards and what their duties were:

'The nurses are all distributed into wards. The medical men in charge of wards apply to me when they want nurses. I refer the application to the first class staff surgeon of the division, and with his permission I send a nurse or nurses, of whom I have the selection. The general nature of their duties they learn from my orders. The patients to whom they are to attend are indicated to them by the medical officer; also the treatment of those patients. They are employed chiefly among the wounded, the operation cases, and the severe medical cases. Their duties among the surgical cases are, to go round in the morning, to wash and prepare such wounds for the medical officers as those officers direct, to attend the medical officers in their dressings, and receive and bring to me those officers' directions as to the diets, drinks, and medical comforts of those cases. They generally go out in fours. A quartett had generally a corridor and two wards of surgical cases. In the medical divisions the nurse's or nurses' duty is to take such cases as the medical officer confides to her. Her business is chiefly to see that the food is properly cooked and properly administered, that the extra diet rolls made on me are attended to, and that cleanliness, as far as possible, of the wards and persons is attended to, and bed sores dressed.'

14 The 10th November marks the end of the first part of Sarah Anne's journal. Up till then she had kept a day-by-day diary—though later she added a few retrospective comments. After 10th November the amount of work and the stress and strain of nursing under these terrible conditions prevented her doing more than jotting down notes and impressions from time to time. Subsequently she put these into narrative form, but precise dating was, more often than not, forgotten.

15 Frances Magdalen Taylor, a Lady Volunteer in Mary Stanley's party, commented that the nurses themselves suffered from want of proper food.

16 These orderlies were members of the ill-fated Ambulance Corps which had been formed from volunteer pensioners. On their arrival at Varna General Hospital in July the members of the Corps walked straight into a cholera epidemic and from then on nothing went right as they were constantly sick, drunk, or too feeble to do their work.

17 Cholera has been endemic in Asia for centuries. In 1831 the disease reached England and a number of epidemics occurred over the next half century or so. The distinction between Asiatic and European forms is really artificial as both are caused by the same micro-organism, *Vibrio cholerae*. The difference in clinical manefestations depends largely on environment—climate, state of sanitation—and the population—degree of malnutrition, general state of health. In any epidemic some patients will collapse and die in a few hours; others will suffer no more than a passing gastrointestinal upset. The mortality rate from the untreated disease is about 60%. The disease at Scutari was viewed rather differently by Margaret Goodman and by Sister Mary Aloysius: 'the sufferings of those attacked did not appear to be so great as that of many cases I had witnessed in England, though death ensued more quickly' (Margaret Goodman).

'The cholera was of the very worst type—the attacked man lasted only four or five hours. Oh! those dreadful cramps; you might as well try to bend a piece of iron as to move the joints' (Sister Aloysius).

18 Although the cause (bacteria) of wound infection was still unknown, it was appreciated that infection could be spread from patient to patient.

Hence the doctor's banning of a sponge and Sarah Anne's use of tow which she destroyed after each dressing.

19 Lady Stratford Canning was the wife of the British Ambassador in Constantinople, Stratford Canning, first Viscount Stratford de Redcliffe.

20 Many years later after she had read Sister Aloysius' book, Sarah Anne commented: 'Sister Mary Aloysius says, in her Appendix, that the Scutari Barracks were capable of holding 5,000 men, and that the General Hospital held 2,000 men. If so, I have quite undercalculated the numbers.'

Sarah Anne had not miscalculated; her figures were quite accurate. Sister Aloysius' figure of 5,000 would more correctly apply to the number of beds in the whole area (five hospitals including the two at Scutari). The Barrack Hospital at its most overcrowded held nearly 2,000 patients.

21 A blister was raised on the skin with a plaster containing a suitable irritant substance such as Spanish fly. The idea behind the practice, which dates from antiquity, was to rid the body of evil humours through the blister fluid. Alternatively, it may be viewed as a form of counter-irritation —giving the patient something else to think about.

22 This form of gangrene, which was quite common, was due to the combined effects of dysentery and cold. The circulation to the feet began to fail owing to the debilitating effect of persistent diarrhoea; cold—of a degree which would have caused no trouble in healthy men—completed the failure and gangrene (the feet turning black) was the result.

23 A cousin of Queen Victoria. His horse had been shot from under him at Inkerman.

24 The German Deaconesses were a group of Protestant nurses founded by Pastor Theodor Fliedner and his wife Friederike in 1833 at Kaiserswerth. They made a great impression on Florence Nightingale, who visited Kaiserswerth twice, in 1850 and 1851.

25 Medical students.

26 This was the Hospitals Commission. There were, in fact, only two doctors (Cumming and Laing) and a lawyer (Maxwell). Dr. Spence had originally been selected, but while awaiting Mr. Maxwell's arrival had decided to visit the Crimea and had been drowned in *Prince*. Dr. Laing was then chosen as his replacement.

27 Sister Elizabeth's examination by the Commissioners was not a trial, simply an attempt to arrive at the truth. In her letter to *The Times* she had overstated the facts and admitted as much in her evidence (Hospitals Commission, p. 329). Florence Nightingale confirmed that Sister Elizabeth had exaggerated the number of deaths (Hospitals Commission, p. 331).

Nevertheless, 'As she [Sister Elizabeth] truly said when we again met, though she was grieved that in a moment of excitement she had been inexact, God in His mercy had brought good out of evil; for many boxes arrived with the address she had desired, whose contents relieved hundreds of suffering soldiers.' (Margaret Goodman, 1862; p. 114.)

28 Alexander Maclean was from Thurso where he had been born, the son of a blacksmith, on July 6, 1832. He qualified to practise medicine with the Licentiateship of the Royal College of Surgeons of Edinburgh in 1853. This served him throughout most of his career for he did not graduate from his university, Aberdeen, until 1884; he proceeded M.D. a year later. Meantime, in 1882, he had become a Fellow of the Royal College. Despite this apparent evidence of late starting, such was not the case. The determination and moral courage he displayed at Scutari (he had been evacuated, sick, from Balaclava on October 31, 1854) served him well during the Indian Mutiny (1857–8) where he was present at a number of sieges and battles. He went on to teach at the Medical School at Hyderabad. In 1861 he was appointed Professor of Military Medicine at the new Army Medical School at Fort Pitt, Chatham, where he lectured eloquently and with the authority of experience on the horrors of such diseases as yellow fever and cholera. He retired from the Army Medical Department on half pay with the honorary rank of Deputy Surgeon General in 1879, and from his chair at the Army Medical School in 1885. On his return to Caithness, he took an active part in local politics and became a J.P. of the county and a County Councillor. He died at Thurso on February 17, 1898.

About the death of Dr. Mackenzie, Sarah Anne later commented: 'Dr. R. Mackenzie died of cholera in the camp just after the battle of Alma. He had done many operations, and returning to his tent could, I think, get only a little salt fish for supper. The pangs of cholera came on, he said "a warm bath might save me". Sir Colin Campbell, afterwards Lord Clyde, had ordered "all lights out", but hearing Dr. R. Mackenzie had cholera, said, of course he might have a light in his tent.'

29 Kulilee (Kuleli, Koulali—it has a variety of spellings) was a few miles further north up the Bosphorus from Scutari. Its cavalry barracks and hospital provided about 750 more beds. Conditions there became appalling and the mortality rate soon exceeded that at the Barrack Hospital.

30 Miss Tebbut. She eventually became Superintendent of the General Hospital.

31 Sister Aloysius said that the nuns received letters from the War Office accusing them of interfering with the religion of Protestant soldiers. 'It is not our way to force the conscience of anyone', she wrote (pp. 55–56). 'Even if we had never promised the War Office not to interfere with them, the Protestant soldiers had been quite safe. The Holy Spirit alone can enlighten the soul.'

32 Mrs. Shaw Stewart (Mrs. was a courtesy title). She was a woman of social standing who had had nursing experience.

33 This was at the end of January 1855, the same time as the hospital at Kulilee was taken over.

34 Probably typhus.

35 Many years later Sarah Anne wrote, 'I find that he and his wife still survive, having brought up a large family, all now grown up and filling good and respectable positions. He has now retired on account of failing health.'

36 Rev. the Hon. Sidney Godolphin Osborne. He came out, with Sidney Herbert's permission, to investigate conditions in the hospitals. His reports were mostly sweeping generalizations that did not stand up very well under cross-examination by the Hospitals Commission or the Roebuck Committee.

37 Mr. Augustus Stafford, M.P., went out to Scutari as a self-appointed critic. The same comments apply to his reports as to those of Mr. Osborne (see note 36).

38 '. . . I wish Miss Nightingale and the ladies would tell these poor noble wounded and sick men that *no-one* takes a warmer interest or feels *more* for their sufferings than their Queen. Day and night she thinks of her beloved troops. So does the Prince.' (Woodham-Smith, p. 196.) This message was contained in a letter written by the Queen on December 4 to Sidney Herbert.

39 See the section in Setting the Scene on 'The army doctors and their hospitals' (pp. 43–5).

40 See note 38.

41 Lord Napier and Ettrick was the Secretary of the British Embassy at Constantinople.

42 Mary Stanley, disillusioned by conditions at the Barrack Hospital, had gone to the hospital at Kulilee when this opened and had tried to run it along lines of her own; she failed miserably.

BIBLIOGRAPHY

Aloysius, Sister Mary. *Memories of the Crimea*. London; Burns and Oates. 1897.

Cantlie, N. *A History of the Army Medical Department*, 2 vols. Edinburgh and London; Churchill Livingstone. 1974.

Dixon, N. F. *On the Psychology of Military Incompetence*. London; Cape. 1976.

Goodman, Margaret. *Experiences of an English Sister of Mercy*. London; Smith, Elder. 1862.

Goodman, Margaret. *Sisterhoods in the Church of England : with Notices of some Charitable Sisterhoods in the Romish Church*. London; Smith, Elder. 1863.

Griffin, G. J. and Griffin, Joanne K. *History and Trends of Professional Nursing*, 7th ed. St. Louis; Mosby. 1973.

Jameson, Mrs. (Anna Brownell). *Sisters of Charity Catholic and Protestant, Abroad and at Home*. London; Longman, Brown, Green, and Longmans. 1855.

(A) Lady Volunteer. *Eastern Hospitals and English Nurses; The Narrative of Twelve Months' Experience in the Hospitals of Koulali and Scutari*. In 2 vols, 2nd ed. London; Hurst and Blackett. 1856.

Nightingale, Florence. *Notes on Matters Affecting the Health, Efficiency, and Hospital Administration of the British Army, Founded Chiefly on the Experience of the Late War*. London; Harrison. 1858.

Nightingale, Florence. *Notes on Nursing. What it is and what it is not*. 1859. With a new introduction by Joan M. E. Quixley. Glasgow and London; Blackie. 1974.

Nutting, M. Adelaide and Dock, Lavinia L. *A History of Nursing*. 2 vols. New York and London; Putnam. 1907.

Report [of the Commission] upon the State of the Hospitals of the British Army in the Crimea and Scutari. London; Eyre and Spottiswoode. 1855. (The Hospitals Commission.)

Report of the Commissioners Appointed to Inquire into the Regulations Affecting the Sanitary Condition of the Army, the Organization of Military Hospltals, and the Treatment of the Sick and Wounded; with Evidence and Appendix. London; Eyre and Spottiswoode. 1858. (The Royal Sanitary Commission.)

Bibliography

Reports from the Select Committee on the Army before Sebastopol; with the Proceedings of the Committee. (First, Second, Third, Fourth, and Fifth Reports; 3 vols. with Index vol.) London; printed by order of the House of Commons. 1855. (The Roebuck Committee.)

Selected Writings of Florence Nightingale. Compiled by Lucy R. Seymer. New York; Macmillan. 1954.

Seymer, Lucy R. *A General History of Nursing.* 3rd ed. London; Faber and and Faber. 1954.

Woodham-Smith, Cecil. *Florence Nightingale.* London; Constable. 1950.

SELECTIVE INDEX

Index

Index